HAPPY HALLOWEEN!

Hundreds of Perfect Party Recipes, Delightful Decorating Ideas & Awesome Activities

Terrance Zepke

Safari Publishing

All queries should be directed to www.safaripublishing.net

Library of Congress Cataloging-in-Publication Data

Zepke, Terrance

Happy Halloween! Hundreds of Perfect Party Recipes, Delightful Decorating Ideas & Awesome Activities/Terrance Zepke p. cm.

ISBN: 978-0-9907653-0-1

1. Halloween. 2. Party Planning, Halloween. 3. Holiday Decorating, Halloween. 4. Party Games, Halloween. 5. Party Recipes, Halloween. I. Title.

First edition

10 9 8 7 6 5 4 3 2 1

Cover design by Sara Whitford

Happy Halloween! Hundreds of Perfect Party Recipes, Delightful Decorating Ideas & Awesome Activities

About the Author

Terrance Zepke has lived and traveled all over the world during her career as a travel writer. She has been to every continent and enjoyed all kinds of adventures, such as exploring hundreds of haunted places and attractions, as well as participating in many ghost investigations. She grew up in the South Carolina Lowcountry, which is full of haunted places and "haints." Terrance has a B. A. in Journalism and a M.A. in Mass Communications from USC. She studied parapsychology at the renowned Rhine Research Center. She is the host of **Terrance Talks Travel**, is in demand as a speaker, and has written hundreds of articles, as well as twenty-eight books. A complete list of her titles is included in the back of this book and you can also find out more about this author and her books at www.terrancezepke.com and www.terrancetalkstravel.com

Introduction

The only thing I enjoy more than poking around haunted houses, cemeteries, and asylums is a good Halloween party. *The music! The food! The decorations! The costumes! What fun!*

I've been to some great parties, such as the Halloween Asylum Ball at the Trans Alleghany Lunatic Asylum, an underground party in London (England), the Witches Ball at the Hawthorne Hotel and Haunted Happenings in Salem, Massachusetts.

But I've also stayed at home and hosted some memorable parties (some admittedly better than others). I'll never forget when my best friend, Denise, and I co-hosted a Halloween party. We were nineteen and decided impulsively (two days before!) it would be fun to have a big party. We called our friends to let them know and counted on the campus "grapevine" to get the word out. First, I cut myself cutting up a sheet to create a ghost to hang in the front window. We set off the fire alarm when we burned our roasted pumpkin seeds. Denise's graveyard cake turned out lopsided. We ran out of food and drinks two hours into the party. I didn't know you need to look for "washable" on the label, so it took several days for my monster make-up to fade. I developed a new appreciation for my mom after gutting my first pumpkin. She always made it look so easy to carve a pumpkin. Obviously, she did most of the work before we got involved. It took me nearly four hours to gut, clean, design, and carve the giant pumpkin we had gotten.

I've learned a lot since then. I've learned all kinds of shortcuts and tricks and I've compiled them into this handy resource. The reason most people don't have parties is because they're so much work. But they don't have to be. It's so easy and affordable to have a spooktacular Halloween party—for adults or kids.

I have included all the information you'll need to (1) plan your party and menu, (2) decorate inside and out, and (3) all kinds of awesome activities suitable for all ages so that your party is a huge hit. It'll be super fun without a lot of fuss—I promise!

Plus, I have provided dozens of resources (such as where to get coffin couches, glow sticks, and free pumpkin stencil kits) and a list of the most haunted houses and best family attractions in America, as well as a history of Halloween complete with lots of fun trivia. This adds up to hundreds of helpful listings.

Remember that the most important thing is to have fun. There is no wrong or right way to do things. Use my decorating tips as guidelines or follow them to the letter. The same is true for recipes, crafts, and games.

For more information about my ghost books, to subscribe to my *MOSTLY GHOSTLY* blog, or to check out **Ghost Town**, visit www.terrancezepke.com.

PARTY PLANNING

Let me start by making a confession. I am not Rachel Ray or Martha Stewart nor do I want to be. I don't enjoy constructing intricate craft projects or slaving away for hours creating elaborate recipes. That said, I love Halloween decorations and party food, so I have learned how to make everything look impressive and taste delicious without having to do a massive amount of work.

The key to a stress-free and successful party is KISS (Army motto: *Keep It Simple, Stupid!*). This means doing everything the KISS way from simple recipes to easy DIY decorations.

Before I discuss the menu options, I want to give you a timeline to help you stay on track. I suggest marking all of this on your calendar right now and then you won't lose track of time or tasks.

 **TIMELINE**

*4 weeks out:

Sort out your costume. Go ahead and buy it, borrow it, rent it, or make it, as soon as possible so that you have that out of the way.

Decide on the date and time for your party. Check your calendar to make sure it is not on a date that conflicts with something big, such as an election, a big football game, festival, school function, wedding, or holiday.

Make a guest list and decide how you're going to notify guests, i.e. paper invitations you'll mail out (see below), e-vites, tweets, and/or by a Facebook post. You may want to have some fun with it by making a two-minute YouTube video of you creating a Halloween decoration while inviting folks to your party or by sharing an Instagram of you in your costume along with a party invite. To encourage folks to wear costumes, be sure to let your guests know there will be a costume contest with a great prize or prizes for funniest, most unusual, and creepiest. Add that to your list so you don't forget to round up prizes. Be sure to give your guests plenty of notice. Fall is a busy time for most folks with lots of festivals and football games. Ask for RSVPs so you can plan to have enough food.

I recommend sending out invites three or four weeks in advance—and be specific. This means that you need to be sure to include location, date, start and end times for the party, if kids are allowed or if you'll have a kid zone (if hosting an adult party), costume and prize information, should a guest bring a food item, parking instructions, etc. You can buy or make your own invitations or find free party invitations online by doing a search. Some options include http://www.printable-greetings.com/?subcategory=41 and www.punchbowl.com.

You can find more options by searching google for "free Halloween invitations." No matter how you invite folks (evites or Facebook or whatever), I recommend following up a week before the party with a phone call or email to those who have not responded. This is a final call to action so that those who may not have seen your invite or forgot about it have a chance to respond. It also helps keep your head count accurate, which is important for knowing how much food and drink you'll need.

Decide what you want to do about food. Do you want to be responsible for all refreshments or would you like guests to bring an item? If so, be specific as to what you'd like the guest to bring, i.e. sub rolls, appetizer, soda, or dessert. I went to a party last year and the host didn't specify. All the guests came with desserts! The host served ham and roast beef but there was nothing else but a table full of sweet treats.

It is much easier and cheaper if guests bring items rather than the host try to provide everything. But if you would prefer not to ask guests to bring items then you may want to think about using catering services, such as ordering a deli tray from your local grocery store or buying rolls from a local bakery.

Figure out your budget. How much can you afford to spend? If you have a small budget, you definitely need to ask guests to bring a dish. Most people don't like to show up empty-handed to a party so they won't mind. What about beverages? Will you serve alcoholic beverages? If so, that can be expensive. How much you need will depend on how many guests you'll be having. The minimum you can get away with is a few cases of beer and some kind of punch, as well as one or two non-alcoholic options like bottled water, coffee or cider, and soda.

Another option is to not have guests bring

anything but charge admission, such as $5 or $10pp. I'm not in favor of this tactic. However, it is your party and you should do whatever you are most comfortable suggesting to your friends and neighbors.

*2 – 4 weeks out:

Buy plastic utensils, napkins, toothpicks, cups, plates, cupcake holders, sprinkles, food coloring, bowls and tablecloth. Make sure all these items are Halloween theme and buy what you need at the dollar store or party shop to save money. Borrow or buy a punch bowl and any other items you need to display or serve food.

Make and/or buy decorations, prizes, and crafts. Before you set out, make a list of what prizes you'll be awarding and what kind of decorations you want to make and then proceed to make a list of where you can get these items.

Decorate as far in advance as possible as this activity is the most time consuming and something you can do well in advance. Also, you'll realize you need more of this or that as you go along and decorating in advance allows you time to pick up additional supplies and get more creative. I tend to get carried away so I like to get started early. It gives me time to rearrange and finalize decorations (including great ideas that inevitably come to me after I've started a project). It also allows me to fully enjoy the fruits of my labors.

*1 week out:

Finalize your menu. Sit down and select a couple of items from each category in Section II of this book. Be sure to take the list of ingredients with you to the store to make sure you get everything you need.

Go shopping! It's time to buy the food and drinks (see above). Use RSVPs to determine how much food you'll need. Plan on too much food and beverages as it is always better to be safe than sorry.

TIP: Expect each guest to consume about a dozen appetizers and desserts. For a dinner party the total would be about half that amount. Guests typically consume two drinks during the first hour of the party and average one for every hour after that. I have included recipes for some specialty punches/brews and recommend mixing up a batch of one of these as it will be much cheaper than offering mixed drinks.

Make/bake and refrigerate/freeze or put food into canisters. Do this with all items you can prepare in advance.

Make sure all decorations work properly. Does everything work like it should, such as light up, spin, dance, speak, and/or sing. Buy batteries, extension cords, and/or replacement lights, as needed.

*Day of Party:

Put up last minute decorations, if applicable. There may something you couldn't do until this point, such as blowing up balloons, but hopefully you have pretty much finished your decorating.

Finish any cooking and baking you need to do. Make sure you thaw anything you need to, warm up whatever you need to, frost or decorate as needed, etc.

Buy ice. Make sure your cooler is wiped out and ready.

Do any last minute cleaning. This includes putting away any and all valuables/breakables. As the saying goes, it's not a party until something's broken...

If using real candles be sure they are secure and there is no danger of fire. I highly discourage the use of taper candles as they are the most likely to cause a fire. Stick to tea candles and/or votive candles. I also like to use lanterns as they are safe and create a fun effect.

If you're going to permit smoking, be sure to have a designated smoking area that is well posted as a "DESIGNATED SMOKING AREA." It should include seating, lighting, and some kind of trash can/ash tray. If you know a lot of smokers, you might want to add some decorations to make it more festive.

Make sure music is playing by the time the party starts and have back up discs or playlists cued for the rest of night. You can find Halloween songs (such as Monster Mash and Ghostbusters), creepy sounds (ghost moaning, screaming, creaking door, witch cackling, and thunder/rain/storm), Halloween stories/tales, and generic party tunes online and in dollar stores.

Get games and prizes ready. Have a list to serve as a guide so you don't have to think about what activities you want to do or when or what prizes you'll award during your party. Let the party find its rhythm before you initiate any games. Give all your guests a chance to arrive and get something to eat and drink and mingle beforehand.

If you have pets, you may want to secure them for the night. You don't want your cat or dog getting loose or spooked or overfed. My doggie is adorable and guests love to feed him but he is on a special diet and had to go to the emergency vet after some well-meaning guests slipped him treats during a party a few years ago. Make sure you have taken your doggie out to do his business, fed the cat, etc. before guests arrive.

Have a designated area where guests can safely leave their belongings, such as purses, coats, phones, etc. throughout the party.

Put food and beverages on separate tables to help with crowd flow. Be sure to allow time for defrosting and/or heating time. Set a timer or stay close so you don't get distracted and forget something in the oven, which is easy to do during a party. Don't put all your food and drinks out at once. Check the tables every half hour or hour and then add one or two more items so as not to run out of food and drinks early in the evening.

Get your costume on and get ready to have fun!

PARTY RECIPES

Food is the key to any successful party. I have included unique recipes that will have party goers praising you (with their mouths full). It is important to have a well-rounded selection, so I have included some great recipes for light and heavy appetizers, desserts, and Halloween theme alcoholic and non-alcoholic drinks.

The most important thing to remember is that guests will usually eat more than you anticipate. So plan to have double what you think you'll need. Don't put everything out at once or it will get gone fast. Keep adding items every forty minutes or before and after games.

You want to have tasty options that don't require a lot of prep or handling. The following recipes fit the bill beautifully. My advice is to make less of the more intricate recipes that create an impressive presentation but are time tedious, such as Frankenstein cookies and Harry Potter cauldrons and more of the easy recipes, such as Reese's cupcakes and Kookie Cookies. This way you have a nice presentation without having to over-exert yourself.

Remember that you're in charge. If you're pressed for time or challenged in the kitchen, stick to the easiest recipes or buy store bought cookie dough, bakery cake, and cupcakes and then add your own special touches, such as whipped topping and gummy spiders or Peeps® marshmallow ghosts or pumpkins (see image) on top of some of the cupcakes and chocolate shavings and Halloween sprinkles on the rest. Use dollar store Halloween cookie cutters to create fun designs using the store bought cookie dough. In a pinch, buy ready-made items and then think of creative ways to display them, such as cupcakes on tiered cupcake stand with plastic or pipe cleaner spiders hanging off the stand and/or a raven attached to the top, etc. You can buy so much cool stuff at the dollar store these days. For other items, such as cupcake stands and punch bowls, borrow from a friends, family member, or neighbor or make the investment for future parties.

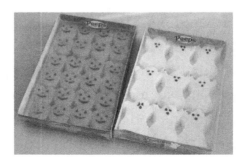

Peanut Butter Rice Krispies Balls

Ingredients (Makes 60 balls):

4 tablespoons margarine or butter
4 1/2 cups miniature marshmallows
1/2 cup + 2 tablespoons peanut butter
6 cups Rice Krispies cereal
Melting chocolate

Melt butter in saucepan over medium heat. Add
marshmallows. Stir 'til melted. Remove from heat. Add

peanut butter, stirring until well mixed. Add Rice Krispies. Let cool for 10 minutes.

Make into 1-inch balls. Melt chocolate according to directions. Dip balls. Let chocolate dry and harden before putting away. You can use milk chocolate, dark chocolate, white chocolate, or a combination thereof.

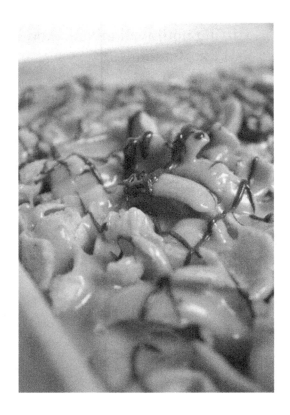

Kookie Cookies

(Also known as Peanut Butter & Corn Chip No Bake Cookies)

Ingredients:

1 package (9.75 to 10.5 ounces) corn chips
1 cup light corn syrup
1 cup sugar
1 cup creamy peanut butter

Spread corn ships in a greased 15 inch x 10 inch by 1 inch baking pan.

In a saucepan over medium heat, bring corn syrup and sugar to a boil, stirring frequently to help dissolve the sugar. Boil 1 minute.

Remove from heat; stir in peanut butter until smooth.

Pour mixture over corn chips.

Drizzle melted semi-sweet chocolate chips over the top.

Let cool and then tear gooey, yummy sweet into pieces. This may sound like a strange combination but the crunchy, salty corn chips are an excellent mix with the sweet ingredients and peanut butter.

Warning: These are addictive!

Candy Bar Dip Recipe

Ingredients:

1 (8-ounce) package cream cheese, softened

½ cup butter, softened

1 teaspoon vanilla

1 cup powdered sugar

2 tablespoons brown sugar

1 cup chocolate chips

1 cup coconut flake

½ cup slivered almonds

Blend cream cheese and butter until smooth mixture.

Add in vanilla and sugars and beat until creamy.

Stir in chocolate chips, coconut and almonds.

Spoon into a serving bowl and top with more chocolate chips, coconut and almonds so it makes a pretty presentation.

Refrigerate until ready to serve.

Serve with pretzel rods or graham crackers.

Optional: Use food color to dye the cream cheese orange or green or add Halloween sprinkles on top.

Chocolate Chip Cookie Frankensteins
(Makes 20; double recipe for 40 monster cookies)

Ingredients:

1 pkg (16oz.) chocolate chip cookie dough bar

1 1/2 cups powdered sugar

2 tablespoons water

Green food coloring

2/3 cup semi-sweet chocolate mini morsels plus additional for "bolts"

40 White Chocolate Pieces or Morsels (for the eyes)

Chocolate and orange sprinkles

Prevent oven to 325° F. Grease and flour 40 mini-muffin cups. Cut dough into squares. Place one square into each cup.

Bake for 10 to 13 minutes or until light golden brown. Cool for 10 minutes in pans on wire racks. Run knife around edge of cups; remove cups to wire racks to cool completely.

Melt 2/3 cup mini morsels in uncovered, microwave-safe bowl on HIGH power for 45 seconds or until completely melted and then stir. Spread melted chocolate on top of one cup; top with second cup. Press down slightly. Return to wire rack. Repeat with remaining cups for a total of 20. These are the heads. Let stand for 15 minutes or until set.

While waiting for that to cool, cut ends off of 40 white morsels to make flat for the eyes. To make pupils, dip toothpick into melted chocolate and make a small dots on bottoms of morsels.

Put a piece of wax paper under wire rack. Combine powdered sugar and water in small bowl. Add food coloring to desired green color. The glaze will be slightly thin, not spreadable like a frosting. Hold each head by seam and dip top cup into glaze. Return to wire rack to allow glaze to drip down over bottom cup. Repeat with others. Additional glaze can be spooned over the tops if needed. While glaze is still wet, sprinkle tops with sprinkles and press down lightly.

Take two morsel eyes and press onto glaze on top cup. For "bolts" use two mini morsels and lightly press onto side of bottom cup, using glaze for glue if needed.

Warning: Until the glaze is completely set, the eyes may slide, so watch carefully and just put back into place. Allow to set completely before attempting to move 'monsters'.

Pumpkin Cream Cheese Cupcakes

(Makes two dozen; double recipe to make four dozen cupcakes)

Ingredients:

3/4 cup butter, softened

2-1/2 cups sugar

3 eggs

1 can (15 ounces) solid-pack pumpkin

2-1/3 cups all-purpose flour

1 tablespoon pumpkin pie spice

1 teaspoon baking powder

1 teaspoon ground cinnamon

3/4 teaspoon salt

1/2 teaspoon baking soda

1/2 teaspoon ground ginger

1 cup buttermilk

FROSTING:

1 package (8 ounces) cream cheese, softened

1/2 cup butter, softened

4 cups powdered sugar

1 teaspoon vanilla extract

2 teaspoons ground cinnamon

Preheat oven to 350°.

In a large bowl, cream butter and sugar until light and fluffy.

Add eggs, one at a time, beating well after each addition.

Add pumpkin.

Combine the flour, pie spice, baking powder, cinnamon, salt, baking soda, and ginger. Add to the creamed mixture while alternately adding the buttermilk, beating well after each addition.

Fill paper-lined muffin cups three-fourths full. Bake for 20-25 minutes or until a toothpick inserted in the center comes out clean.

Cool for 10 minutes before removing from pans to wire racks to cool completely.

For frosting: in a large bowl, beat cream cheese and butter until fluffy. Add powdered sugar, cinnamon, and vanilla; beat until smooth. Frost cupcakes. Insert plastic Halloween theme toothpicks in each cupcake (dollar store).

Reese's Chocolate Chip Brownies

Ingredients:

Chocolate Chip Cookie Dough Bar

Large size peanut butter cups

Brownie Mix

Preheat oven to 350 degrees.

Make brownie mix according to directions on the box.

Spray each square of pan with cooking spray.

Scoop big tablespoon of cookie dough & press into bottom of each square.

Top cookie dough with an upside down Reese's Peanut Butter Cup.

Fill the rest of the square with brownie mix.

Bake for 15 minutes. Remove & sprinkle w/Halloween sprinkles or can frost (or drizzle) w/ orange icing.

This is a great dessert for chocolate lovers! We're talking death by chocolate!

Mummy Cookie Balls

Ingredients (makes 48 mini mummies):

1 pkg. (8 oz.) cream cheese, softened

36 OREO® Cookies or Golden OREO® Cookies, finely crushed

3-1/2 pkg. (4 oz. each) White Chocolate (14 oz.)

Chocolate sprinkles, miniature semi-sweet chocolate chips or anything you like to decorate

Mix cream cheese and cookie crumbs until blended.

Make into 1-inch balls. Freeze 10 min.

Melt 12 oz. white chocolate as directed on package.

Dip balls in melted chocolate; place in single layer on waxed paper-covered rimmed baking sheet. (Re-freeze balls if they become too soft to dip.) Refrigerate 1 hour or until firm.

Melt remaining chocolate as directed on package; spoon into small plastic bag and seal. Cut 1/8-inch piece from one bottom corner of bag. Squeeze bag to pipe chocolate onto each ball for the mummy's eyes; immediately add decorations for the eyeballs. Pipe remaining chocolate onto balls to resemble gauze strips. Refrigerate until firm. Can be made in advance and stored in refrigerator until the party.

Reese's Cupcakes

Ingredients:

White or yellow cake mix

Reese's Pieces®

Use any brand yellow or white cake mix (I like Pillsbury with pudding in the mix). Make according to directions and then add Reese's pieces®.

Optional: Add chocolate or orange frosting, but they are so tasty and pretty that it's not necessary. So easy!

Candy Corn Pizza

Ingredients:

1 roll (16.5 oz.) refrigerated sugar cookies

½ cup creamy peanut butter

1 cup candy corn

½ cup raisins or craisins

¼ cup whipped white or vanilla ready-to-spread frosting (from can)

Cover a 12-inch pizza pan with foil (be sure to use cooking spray on the foil). Cut cookie dough into 1/4-inch-thick slices and arrange in pan. With floured fingers, press slices so as to form a crust. Bake at 350°F

37

for 15 to 20 minutes or until golden brown. Cool completely. Carefully remove foil from crust and place crust on a serving platter or tray. Spread peanut butter (I like to use honey peanut butter but can be plain or even crunchy peanut butter) over crust. Sprinkle candy corn and raisins evenly over top. Or you can use other toppings as well or in place of, such as chocolate or butterscotch chips or slivered almonds. In small microwavable bowl, microwave frosting on High for no more than 10 to 15 seconds (should be thin so that you can drizzle it over cookie pizza). Wait five minutes and then cut into party-sized wedges or squares.

Tip: You can buy a giant premade cookie at most grocery store bakeries and simply add the toppings. Or you can ask someone in the bakery to decorate it for you by adding a fun Halloween greeting in black and some Halloween sprinkles and piping the outer edge with orange icing. They will usually do this at no extra charge or for a small fee.

Harry Potter Chocolate Cauldrons

(Makes 12 cauldrons; double recipe to make two dozen)

Ingredients:

12 Devil's Food cupcakes
Chocolate glaze (see below)
Marshmallow filling (see below)
1/2 cup chocolate chips
Edible gold glitter

Chocolate Glaze
6 ounces (1 cup) semi-sweet chocolate chips
4 tablespoons butter

In a double boiler, melt together the chocolate and butter, stirring until smooth. Glaze will be relatively thick. Remove from heat and let sit 5 minutes before use. If chocolate thickens too much, return to heat and stir until smooth and melted once more.

Marshmallow Filling
1 cup marshmallow fluff or cream
1/2 cup vegetable shortening
1/2 cup confectioners' sugar
2 teaspoons vanilla extract

In a medium bowl, beat together the marshmallow fluff, shortening, sugar, and vanilla extract until light and fluffy, about 3-5 minutes.

To Create Cauldron
Use a sharp knife to cut out a cavity in the *bottom* of the cupcake. When using a knife, I run it in a circular motion around the cupcake, while always pointing the knife towards the center (this will make the cavity cone shaped).

Dip the top of the cupcake into the chocolate glaze. Flip the cupcakes right side up and let rest until the chocolate sets, about 30 minutes. To speed up the process, place cupcakes in the refrigerator.

To make the cauldron feet, take 3 chocolate chips and form a small triangle, placing each chocolate chip roughly an inch from the others. Place the top of a cupcake onto the chocolate chips and push down ever so slightly so the chocolate chips will stick into the chocolate glaze. Repeat for the rest of the cupcakes.

Place remaining chocolate glaze into a piping bag and pipe a chocolate rim around the edge of the opening to the cauldron. If chocolate is too thick to pipe, heat chocolate glaze up until warm and allow to sit until glaze thickens slightly. If chocolate glaze is too runny to pipe, wait a few minutes until the glaze thickens to a pipe-able consistency. Alternatively, you could use a knife to spread the glaze around the edge of the cupcake.

Fill a pastry bag with marshmallow filling and pipe into the cavity of the cupcakes. Garnish the top with edible gold glitter.

To make cauldron handle, melt the remaining chocolate chips, stir until smooth, and place into a pastry bag. You don't need a special tip for this step; I simply cut off the very end of the pastry bag which was sufficient. On a non-stick mat or wax paper, pipe out the handles (feel free to use any pattern you'd like). I recommend measuring the cupcakes with a ruler to determine how wide you need to make the handles *before* piping. Let the chocolate set until hardened, approximately 30 minutes, before very carefully peeling off of the non-stick surface and placing into the top of each cupcake.

Pumpkin Whoopie Pies

Ingredients (makes 16):

1 pkg. (2-layer size) yellow cake mix

1 pkg. (3.4 oz.) Vanilla Flavor Instant Pudding

2 tsp. pumpkin pie spice

1 cup canned pumpkin

1/3 cup oil

1/3 cup water

3 eggs

1 pkg. (8 oz.) cream cheese, softened

1 jar (7 oz.) Marshmallow Crème or Fluff

¼ tsp. ground cinnamon

1 tub (8 oz.) Whipped Topping, room temperature

½ cup Halloween sprinkles

Beat first 7 ingredients with mixer until well blended. Scoop into 32 mounds, 3 inches apart, on baking sheet sprayed with cooking spray, using about 2 tbsp. for each.

Bake at 350°F 12 to 14 min. or until toothpick inserted in centers comes out clean. Cool on baking sheet 2 min. Remove to wire racks; cool completely.

Beat cream cheese, marshmallow cream, ginger and cinnamon in large bowl with mixer until well blended. Whisk in COOL WHIP® (whipped topping). Spread 3 Tbsp. onto flat side of 1 cake; top with second cake, flat-side down. Roll edge in sprinkles. Repeat with remaining cakes. Keep refrigerated.

Swamp Cake

Ingredients

1 pkg. (2-layer size) devil's food cake mix

8 OREO® Cookies, chopped

1 (8 oz.) tub of Whipped Topping, thawed

1-1/4 cups boiling water

2 pkg. (3 oz. each) Lime Flavor Gelatin

2 cups ice cubes

7 Soft & Chewy Candies

1 large Marshmallow

44

5 worm-shaped chewy fruit snacks

½ tsp. black decorating gel

1 piece black licorice

1 Peanut Bar (1.6 oz.), cut into pieces

1 (1.2 oz.) Milk Chocolate bar with Nougat, cut into pieces

Make cake batter and bake in 13x9-inch pan according to directions. Once completely cooled, remove (inverted) from cake pan. Hollow out center of cake, leaving thin layer on bottom and about 2-inch-wide irregular-shaped border on sides. Crumble all the removed cake. Put aside 2 Tbsp. Mix remaining crumbled cake with chopped cookies.

Spread about 1/2 cup whipped topping onto bottom of hole in cake. Add boiling water to gelatin mixes in large bowl; stir 2 min. until completely dissolved. Add ice cubes; stir until gelatin starts to thicken. Stir in the 2 tbsp. cake crumbs you set aside. Spoon over whipped topping in cake. Add chewy candies as shown in photo. Refrigerate 3 hours or until gelatin is firm.

Frost sides and border of cake with remaining whipped topping. Press enough cookie crumb mixture into whipping topping to evenly cover whipped topping. Sprinkle remaining crumb mixture onto platter around cake.

Roll marshmallow into 3-inch-long piece; fold lengthwise in half and flatten slightly to resemble ghost. Place on cake; use decorating gel to make eyes. Decorate cake with remaining ingredients to resemble photo. Feel free to decorate according to whim, meaning you may add additional items (edible candy shaped like bones or tiny signs on toothpicks "Beware!" or "Warning!") or arrange differently.

Keep refrigerated until ready to serve.

I love this idea for a kids' party!

Mini Pumpkin Pies

Ingredients (Makes 48 mini pies)

48 tart shells

1/3 cup granulated sugar
1/4 teaspoon salt
1 1/2 teaspoons pumpkin pie spice
1 cup pure pumpkin puree
1 teaspoon pure vanilla extract
1 5-ounce can evaporated milk
1 canister whipped cream

47

In a medium bowl, mix on low speed: sugar, salt, pumpkin pie spice, egg, pumpkin, vanilla and evaporated milk. Beat until smooth.

Place mini tart shells on prepared baking sheet (lined with parchment paper). Using a small scooper, fill each mini tart shell with pumpkin pie filling.

Put pan into preheated 350°F oven and bake for 15-17 minutes or until shells are golden brown and the filling has set. Let cool and top with whipped cream and Halloween sprinkles or create a monster face on each pie by using chips and sprinkles.

Pumpkin Dump Cake

Ingredients:

4 eggs, beaten
2 cups cooked pumpkin
1 1/2 cups sugar
12 oz. can evaporated milk
1 teaspoon salt
1 teaspoon nutmeg
2 teaspoons cinnamon
1 yellow cake mix
1/2 cup chopped pecans (pecan halves)
2 sticks melted butter

Mix first 8 ingredients together. Pour into a 13x9 inch pan. Sprinkle cake mix evenly over pumpkin mixture.

Sprinkle chopped or pecan halves over the cake mix, then pour melted butter evenly over the cake mix.

Bake at 350 degrees F for 50 minutes - 1 hour or until lightly browned. Serve plain or with whipped topping and Halloween sprinkles on top or you can add small plastic monsters to the top that are available at most dollar store.

Pumpkin Fudge

Ingredients:

2 cups granulated sugar
1 cup packed light brown sugar
3/4 cup (1 1/2 sticks) butter
2/3 cup (5 oz. can) evaporated milk
1/2 cup pumpkin puree
2 teaspoons pumpkin pie spice
2 cups (12 ounce package) white chocolate chips
1 jar (7 oz.) marshmallow crème
1 cup chopped pecans (optional)
1 1/2 teaspoons vanilla extract

Line a 13 x 9-inch baking pan with foil.

In a heavy medium saucepan, combine the sugar, brown sugar, evaporated milk, pumpkin, butter and pumpkin pie spice. Bring to a full rolling boil over medium heat, stirring constantly for 10 to 12 minutes or until candy thermometer reaches 234° to 240° F (soft-ball stage).

Stir in white chocolate chips, marshmallow crème, nuts and vanilla extract and stir vigorously for 1 minute until chips are melted.

Immediately pour into prepared pan. Let stand on wire rack for 2 hours or until completely cooled. Refrigerate tightly cover

To cut, lift foil from pan. Remove foil and cut fudge into 1-inch pieces. Add dollar store spider web over the top or across the bottom of the plate to create spooky effect.

Halloween Party Cake

Ingredients:

1 box white cake mix (I recommend Betty Crocker SuperMoist®
cake mix or Pillsbury® cake mix with pudding

1 box Dark Chocolate cake mix (I recommend Betty Crocker
SuperMoist or Pillsbury with pudding in mix)

Black food coloring

Purple food coloring (better color selections are available
in a specialty shop rather than the grocery store)

Orange food coloring

12 oz. can white frosting (preferably whipped)

Heat oven to 325°F. Grease a 12-cup tube cake pan with cooking spray. Make cakes according to box directions. Divide the white cake into two separate bowls.

Add orange food coloring to one bowl and mix to the desired color. Then, add purple to the other and mix to the desired color.

Pour 2/3 of the chocolate cake batter into a bowl and mix with a few drops of the black food coloring. Do not use all the batter or it won't fit in the pan. You may want to make cupcakes with the rest of the batter.

Pour 1/2 of the chocolate cake mix into the bottom of the greased pan. Slowly pour the purple over the top of the chocolate cake but do NOT stir it.

Next, pour the orange batter over the purple batter and pour in the rest of the chocolate, which is roughly 1/3 or 1/4. Bake as directed on box or until ready. Cool completely and remove from pan.

Divide your frosting into 3 bowls: orange, purple and black. Microwave each bowl for a few seconds on high until it is smooth enough to drizzle over the cake.

Using a spoon, drizzle the black frosting back and forth around the whole ring in a striping pattern until you use it all. Then do the same with the purple and then the orange.

Store loosely covered and unrefrigerated. Cake can be made up to two days in advance.

Easy Ice Cream

Ingredients:

24 Halloween theme cupcake liners (and spoons)

24-count muffin/cupcake pan(s)

Chocolate ice cream

Orange and/or lime sherbet

Ice cream is always a crowd pleaser but often requires too much time for a busy party supervisor. But here's a cool idea for a kids Halloween party that involves NO effort. Freeze individual scoops of chocolate and orange and/or lime sherbet in cupcake liners the night before the party. Remove from freezer and serve! Be sure to add a few festive Halloween sprinkles before putting ice cream "bowls" into freezer.

LIGHT APPETIZERS

Sweet & Salty Roasted Pumpkin Seeds

(Makes 1 - 2 cups or double recipe for 2-3 cups)

Ingredients:

1 1/2 cup rinsed and cleaned whole pumpkin seeds
1 tablespoon olive oil
1/4 cup cinnamon sugar
2 teaspoon kosher salt

Preheat oven to 400°.

Line a half sheet pan with parchment paper.

Add pumpkin seeds, drizzle with olive oil and sprinkle with cinnamon sugar and kosher salt.

Add seeds to oven and after ten minutes stir the nuts. Let the seeds cook for 7-8 minutes longer. Make sure to not let the sugar burn.

Pull the seeds out of the oven, sprinkle with a pinch more of kosher salt and let cool for 10 minutes.

After cool, break the seeds into smaller "chunks."

Pumpkin Pillows

Ingredients (makes 20):

12 caramel cubes

1 tsp. water

½ cup regular or low fat sour cream

1 tsp. ground cinnamon

4 oz. cream cheese, softened

½ cup canned pumpkin

1 tbsp. brown sugar

1 tsp. flour

¼ tsp. orange zest

20 won ton wrappers

1 egg white, lightly beaten

2 cups oil

1tbsp. powdered sugar

Microwave caramels and water in medium microwaveable bowl on HIGH 30 sec.; stir until caramels are completely melted. Cool 2 min. Stir in sour cream and 1/2 tsp. cinnamon. Refrigerate until ready to use.

Beat cream cheese, pumpkin, brown sugar, flour, zest and remaining cinnamon until well blended. Spoon about 2 tsp. onto center of each won ton wrapper. Moisten edges with egg white; fold diagonally in half. Pinch edges together tightly to seal.

Heat oil in large saucepan on medium-high heat to 350°F. Add won tons, in batches; cook 2 to 3 min. or until evenly browned. Drain. Cool slightly or to room temperature. Sprinkle with powdered sugar. Serve with caramel or chocolate sauce (sold in grocery stores on same aisle as ice cream cones and toppings).

Optional: Drizzle green or orange food color around the plate or place a little ghost in the middle of the plate.

Tip: Won ton wrappers dry out quickly so keep covered with damp towel. Can make and refrigerate ahead of time. When time for party, place on baking sheet and bake for 10 – 15 minutes (or until thoroughly heated) at 350°F.

Tasty Bones

Ingredients:

1 pkg. (11 oz.) refrigerated soft breadsticks

¼ cup grated Parmesan Cheese

½ cup ranch dressing

1 tbsp. hot pepper sauce

Heat oven to 375°F.

Cut breadsticks crosswise in half. Take a piece and stretch it until it is five inches. Tie a knot at each end. Roll bread in parmesan cheese until evenly coated.

Cook on baking sheet, approximately two inches apart for about ten minutes or until brown. Let cool and serve.

Mix ranch dressing and pepper sauce until well blended. This is the dipping sauce for the bread bones. Add more pepper sauce if want a spicier dip.

Swamp Dip

Ingredients (Serves 4 – 6):

3 avocados, peeled and cubed (can use frozen or premade guacamole)

2 tablespoons lime juice

1/2 teaspoon salt

1/8 teaspoon pepper

1/3 cup sour cream

1/4 teaspoon tabasco sauce

1 tomato, seeded and chopped

4-6 cups green guacamole chips (blue tortilla chips)

Place avocado in medium bowl; add lime juice, salt, and pepper and mash using a potato masher to desired consistency. Stir in the sour cream, Tabasco sauce, and chopped tomato. Transfer to a serving bowl and surround with guacamole chips or dark blue tortilla chips.

Delicious!

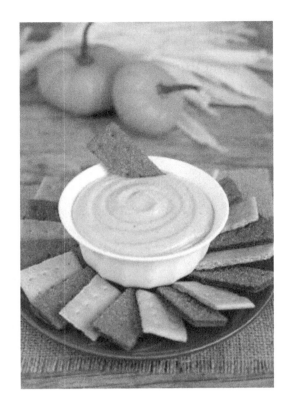

Pumpkin Pie Dip

Ingredients (makes 4 cups):

8 oz. cream cheese, softened

2 cups powdered sugar

1 1/4 cups canned pumpkin

1/2 cup sour cream

1/2 tsp cinnamon

68

1/2 tsp nutmeg

1/2 tsp ginger

1/4 - 1/2 cup caramel sauce, store bought or homemade

crackers

In a large mixing bowl, blend cream cheese and powdered sugar until smooth and fluffy. Fold in pumpkin, sour cream, cinnamon, nutmeg, and ginger and mix until smooth and fluffy. Store in refrigerator in an airtight container until ready to serve. Drizzle with caramel sauce and serve with sweet crackers, such as graham crackers, chocolate wafers, or gingersnap cookies.

Halloween Popcorn Balls

Ingredients:

1 cup sugar

¾ cup margarine

1 ½ cups corn syrup

½ tsp. salt

20 cups popped popcorn

4 cups candy corn (optional)

Orange food coloring

Combine the sugar, margarine, corn syrup, and salt in pan over medium heat. Bring to a boil and stir for two minutes. Remove from heat. Add orange food coloring (enough to turn mixture bright orange). Stir in popcorn and candy corn. Cool slightly (enough so that you can handle them but not so long as to make working with mixture impossible) and then begin shaping into balls about 4 or 5 inches in diameter. Cool on wax paper. Wrap balls individually in Halloween theme plastic wrap.

Tip: Dip hands in cold water before making balls.

Devils Snack Mix

Ingredients:

8 cups of rice, corn, & wheat cereal (or any combination thereof)

1 cup peanuts

1 cup mini cheese crackers (Nabisco Cheese Nips®)

1 package taco seasoning (dry)

6 tbsp. margarine

1 tbsp. Worcestershire sauce

1 tsp hot pepper sauce (optional)

Preheat oven to 250 degrees. Melt margarine in roasting pan. Stir in taco seasoning, Worcestershire sauce, and hot pepper sauce. Then stir in rest of ingredients. Bake for 1 hour, stirring every 10 – 15 minutes. Spread mixture on wax paper or paper towels to cool. Store in airtight container and then serve in Halloween theme bowl or canister or in individual Halloween cupcake holders.

Tip: There are lots of variations on this mix including using pecans, candy corn, cheese curls, and pretzels, depending on your preferences (or what you have on hand). Or you can simply buy a bag of Chex Cereal Mix® that is already assembled and simply empty bad into bowl.

Goblin Mix

1 bag or canister of mixed nuts

1 bag of candy corn

If you want something super easy and cheap but better than putting out a can of nuts, this is a good compromise.

Buy or mix together any combination of nuts you desire. Add a bag of Halloween them candy corn (mini pumpkins in Halloween colors). Toss and store in airtight container. Serve in Halloween theme cupcake holders or a large plastic Halloween bowl.

Tip: You can vary this recipe by substituting Reese's® peanut butter pieces or Halloween M & M's® (I like pretzel M & M's in this recipe) or coconut flakes or whatever you like in lieu of candy corn. Or you can simply add a few chocolate covered peanuts or white chocolate bark pieces to mixed nuts.

Goblin Munch

Ingredients:

4 cups Golden Grahams® cereal

2 cups Cocoa Puffs® cereal

2 cups thin pretzel sticks (2 1/4 inch)

1 cup Reese's Pieces®

1 cup dry-roasted peanuts

10 oz. white chocolate baking bars or squares, chopped

2 tablespoons butter or margarine

½ cup powdered sugar

In large bowl, mix cereals, pretzels, peanut butter candies and peanuts; set aside.

In 1-quart microwavable bowl, microwave white chocolate and butter uncovered on High about 1 minute, stirring once, until melted and chocolate can be stirred smooth. Pour over cereal mixture, stirring until evenly coated.

In large food-storage plastic bag, toss half of the cereal mixture with 1/4 cup of the powdered sugar until evenly coated. Spread on waxed paper to cool. Repeat with remaining cereal mixture and remaining 1/4 cup powdered sugar. Store tightly covered at room temperature.

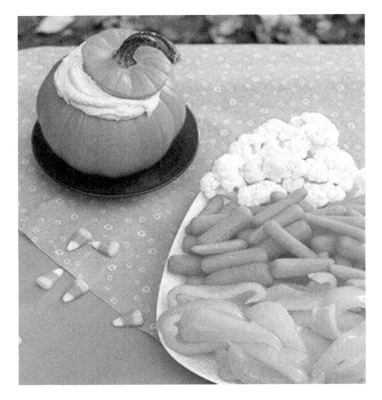

Sweet or tangy dip with vegetables

Ingredients:

Mini pumpkin

12-16 ounces dip

Raw veggies

Make your own favorite dip recipe or use store bought dip. There are lots of great choices in the refrigerator section of most grocery stores.

Using a mini pumpkin, carve an opening at the top, gut it, and make sure the inside is clean and completely dry.

Transfer your bowl or container of dip into the cavity of the pumpkin. Serve with Halloween-colored veggies, such as celery sticks, green pepper strips, and baby carrots.

Tip: If you are pressed for time or simply don't want to clean out even a small pumpkin, you can buy a pumpkin plate/bowl at the dollar store and use it for dip instead. But I do encourage you to buy a mini pumpkin and go for it. They only cost about $2 at most and are so easy to clean and prepare and I think the effort is worth the effect.

HEAVY APPETIZERS

Do you really need heavy appetizers? You may be wondering if you can get away with light appetizers. The answer is NO! You need some solid food to go with the light appetizers and desserts. The good news is that you don't need but one or two of these big guns.

Here are the best choices:

*One option is to have a carving station and serve a ham or roast beef, as well as rolls and spicy horseradish and mustard.

*Instead of a carving station you can have a large deli tray that you made or picked up at the grocery story. Be sure to order at least three days in advance if you choose a pre-made deli tray. You can order a sub tray from a sub shop or deli instead of the grocery store at a cheaper price sometimes.

*Make your own sandwiches. If making the sandwiches yourself, use various types of good quality thinly-sliced meat (I suggest ham, turkey, and roast beef or at least ham and turkey) and cheese (I suggest American or cheddar and swiss) and pimento cheese (vegetarian option).

Optional: Use large sized Halloween cookie cutters (such as witches, bats, and ghosts) to make Halloween sandwiches. Arrange on large Halloween theme tray and have condiments (such as mayonnaise and mustard, onions and/pickles, tomatoes and/or black olives, and salt & pepper) on another tray. I advise skipping lettuce as it's not necessary. If serving mayonnaise, be sure to put ice under container or serve individual packets in iced bowl as it can easily spoil when unrefrigerated. Make plenty of these little sandwiches as they are a crowd pleaser.

*Have a taco, chili, or slider station. In addition to the entree, you can serve all kinds of fun and innovative toppings, depending on whether you go with tacos or chili (onions/cheese/sour cream/tortilla strips) or breaded chicken and/or beef sliders (onions/pickles/cheese/tomatoes/mushrooms/spicy sauce).

I like to serve sliders on tiny potato rolls I find in the bread aisle of the grocery store. Remember that you can serve as much or as few condiments and toppings as you want so if you're on a tight budget stick to the basics: cheese, onions, ketchup, mayo, and mustard.

*Be sure to serve a classic: chicken fingers, peel-and-eat shrimp, pigs in a blanket, or spicy meatballs (see recipe on next page). Just make sure that whatever you choose you buy enough for all your guests. I always serve meatballs as they are a crowd pleaser, super easy, and fairly cheap. I put them in a crock pot on low and they stay warm and tasty all night—or until I run out!

*You can serve stew, soup, and/or a casserole. I have included some suggestions later in this chapter.

Monster Meatballs

Ingredients:

1   jar of grape jelly
1   bottle Heinz Chili Sauce®
One Package of Frozen Meatballs

Mix all ingredients and then cook in Crockpot for 6 hours. Simmer on lowest heat during party and stir periodically.

Tip: You can get frozen meatballs fairly cheap in the freezer aisle of grocery story. But you can also make your own by buying a large container of ground beef on sale (it's always on sale) and then rolling the meat into small balls and cooking/browning in a frying pan on medium heat. You don't need to season the meat since you'll be adding chili sauce and jelly for flavoring. Remember to make the meatballs small (about 1") so they go farther.

Monster Claws

Ingredients:

4 small boneless skinless chicken breasts (1 lb.), cut lengthwise in half (as pictured)

1 pkt. Extra Crispy Seasoned Coating Mix

¼ red pepper, cut into 8 triangular pieces

½ cup teriyaki or barbecue sauce

Roll chicken in coating mix as directed on package. Place on baking sheet sprayed with cooking spray.

Bake at 400°F for 15 min. or until chicken is done.

Make a 1/2-inch slit in the thinner end of each chicken strip; insert a red pepper triangle in slit for the monster's claw. The photo shows you how to arrange claws on plate so as to resemble a monster's hand.

Serve with your favorite homemade dipping sauce or store bought teriyaki or barbecue sauce.

FYI: You can buy severed fingers (and I've seen ears and eyes too) at dollar stores, online, or in Halloween specialty shops, which can be placed on trays alongside real food—if you dare!
www.halloweenexpress.com

Ghoulish Goulash

Ingredients:

1 pounds lean ground beef
1 medium onion, chopped
1 can diced tomatoes
1 small bag frozen whole kernel corn
2 cups uncooked macaroni
1 can beef broth
3 tablespoons chili seasoning
1 tablespoon sugar
1 teaspoon garlic
1 teaspoon dried oregano
1 teaspoon salt
1/2 teaspoon black pepper
1 cup shredded cheddar cheese (optional)
1 cup sour cream (optional)

In a large skillet, brown the ground beef and onion.

Add the remaining ingredients, except cheese, to the skillet and mix well.

Immediately pour mixture into crock pot and cook for 3 1/2 hours on low.

When the goulash is nearly done, turn to lowest heat and put out.

Tip: Like chili, I think that ghoulish is best with grated cheddar cheese and/or sour cream available as toppings. This is a great party dish because it is very filling (in fact, I place Dixie cups next to it rather than bowls) and it is something that you don't often see served at parties so guests will appreciate the novelty. Be sure to put a sign next to the dish to identify it as "Ghoulish Ghoulash."

Pumpkin Bisque

Ingredients:

1 large onion, chopped
2 cloves garlic, chopped
1 tablespoon butter or margarine
1 16-ounce can pumpkin puree
4 cups chicken stock
1/2 teaspoon freshly ground black pepper
1/4 teaspoon ground allspice
1/2 teaspoon sugar
1 cup half-and-half or light cream
1/4 cup dry sherry
grated nutmeg

Sauté the onion and garlic in the butter until they are soft. Add the pumpkin, chicken stock, ground pepper, allspice, sugar, and sherry. Bring to a boil and cover. Simmer the soup for 30 minutes. Place the mixture in a blender and puree until smooth. Return the soup to the pot, add the half-and-half, and simmer until well heated. Garnish with the nutmeg and serve.

This soup can be served either hot or cold but I prefer it hot. It goes great with pumpkin cornbread or pumpkin muffins (see next recipe).

FYI: I like to serve goulash, chili (meat, meatless, or chicken), Brunswick stew, or pumpkin soup at Halloween parties because fall is the perfect season for these dishes. Also, it is cheap per serving as compared to chicken fingers, shrimp, and deli sandwiches. Another good reason I like this recipe is that it satisfies vegetarians and/or those simply trying to eat less meat.

Pumpkin Muffins

Ingredients:

1 large onion, chopped

3/4 cup yellow cornmeal

1 tsp baking powder

½ tsp baking soda

½ tsp pumpkin pie spice

¼ tsp salt

2 eggs, beaten

1 can pumpkin puree

½ cup dark brown sugar

¼ cup pure canola oil

1 cup chopped pecans (optional)

Grease muffin cups or line with paper muffin liners. In a large bowl, stir flour, cornmeal, baking powder, baking soda, and salt and make a well in the center. In a small bowl, stir together the eggs, pumpkin, sugar, and oil. Make a well in the center of the dry ingredients and pour in the egg mixture. Stir just barely blended and then fold in pecans. Divide the batter evenly among prepared muffin tin cups. Bake at 425°F in preheated oven for 15 to 20 minutes or until done. If you insert a toothpick into center of a muffin and it comes out clean, the muffins are done. These muffins go great with the Pumpkin Bisque recipe.

Pumpkin Corn Bread

Ingredients (makes 12 servings):

6 tbsp. butter, melted

2 cups cornmeal

1/3 cup sugar

2 tbsp. corn flour

2 tsp baking powder

1 tsp baking soda

1 tsp salt

1/4 teaspoon pumpkin pie spice

1 cup buttermilk

8 oz. sour cream (nonfat or low fat)

1 egg, lightly beaten

3/4 cup canned pumpkin

whipped butter (optional)

Preheat oven to 350 degrees F. Coat 12-inch cast-iron skillet with 2 tablespoons of the butter; set aside remaining butter.

In a large mixing bowl combine cornmeal, sugar, corn flour, baking powder, baking soda, salt, and pumpkin pie spice. In another bowl combine remaining butter, buttermilk, sour cream, egg, and pumpkin; whisk into cornmeal mixture. Pour into prepared skillet. To make muffins instead of cornbread slices, use muffin pans and cupcake liners. Bake 8-10 minutes or until done. Serves 12-24 depending on whether you make mini-muffins or full-size muffins.

Bake for 20 to 25 minutes or until a toothpick comes out clean. Cool on wire rack; serve warm with whipped butter.

Tip: Prepare and bake as directed. Wrap cooled corn bread in foil. Store in refrigerator up to 2 days. Reheat on 325°F, wrapped in foil (or muffins on 300°F) for 10-15 minutes or until warm. You can serve with or without butter or margarine but I love these with honey butter. Yum!

Monster Meatloaf & Potato Cupcakes

Ingredients (Makes 12 servings; double this recipe to get 24 meat cupcakes):

2 baking potatoes, peeled and quartered

1 1/4 pounds sweet or hot Italian sausage, casings removed (or whatever meat you like, such as hamburger or turkey beef)

1 onion, finely chopped

1 yellow bell pepper, finely chopped

1/2 cup heavy cream

2 tablespoons butter

salt

1 1/4 cups breadcrumbs

2 large eggs, beaten

Preheat the oven to 400 degrees Line a 12-cup muffin pan with foil cupcake liners (paper liners will not be sturdy enough). In a medium saucepan, bring the potatoes to a boil in salted water. Cook until tender, about 15 minutes; drain. While potatoes are boiling, cook the sausage or whatever meat you prefer over medium-high heat for about 5 – 10 minutes. Drain grease and add the onion and bell pepper.

Cook for about five minute until onion and pepper are soft. Using an electric mixer, beat the potatoes, cream, butter and 1/2 teaspoon salt until smooth. Using your hands, combine the breadcrumbs and sausage mixture, breaking up any large pieces. Mix in the eggs; season with 1/2 teaspoon salt. Fill each prepared muffin cup with 1/3 cup sausage mixture. Bake until browned, about 30 minutes. Let cool and transfer to a party platter.

Fill a pastry bag fitted with a star tip (or you can use a plastic food storage bag with a corner cut off) with the mashed potatoes and pipe onto each cupcake.

Tip: This is more labor intensive than other appetizers but like a couple of the dessert options, I think it is worth the effort. These are so filling and unusual. I always get lots of raves from the guys and recipe requests from female guests. Be sure to place a homemade sign next to the plate to identify these cool "Monster Meat and Potato Cupcakes."

Zombie Punch

2 cups 7-Up® or Sprite®
2 cups lime soda
4 cups ginger ale
1 gallon lime sherbet, softened

Place ingredients in punch bowl and stir to blend. This is great beverage for kids or adults. I like to add spooky spider webs and spiders on and around the punch bowl.

Bloody Vampire Punch

1 quart or liter cranberry juice
1 liter 7-Up® or Sprite®
1 pkg. frozen strawberries in syrup, thawed
grenadine (pomegranate syrup)

Place strawberries in punch bowl. Pour cranberry juice, 7-Up or Sprite, and grenadine.

Important: Do not stir!

Tip: You can add fun stuff to this or any punch to make it more festive, such as frozen grapes or other fruit, dry ice or glow sticks, plastic eyeballs, plastic spiders. You can add whatever you like to punch but you need to make sure that any item(s) are big enough that guests can easily see it. You don't want them swallowing anything that wasn't meant to be consumed!

Halloween Sangria

Ingredients:

1 grapefruit, peeled and cut into supreme style segments

2 oranges, peeled and cut into supreme style segments

1 blood orange, cut into slices

2 clementine mandarins, cut into slices

10 kumquats cut into slices

2 tablespoons honey

½ cup orange liqueur like Grand Marnier

2 cups chilled sparkling water

juice of 1 lemon

bottle of chilled Moscato wine (or wine of preference)

Note: For non-alcoholic version, substitute sparkling white grape juice for wine and liqueur

Ice

Put the citrus fruit slices and segments in a pitcher. Add the honey and orange liqueur, let macerate for at least 30 minutes.

Add the chilled sparkling water, Moscato wine, lemon juice and ice. Mix well. The citrus Moscato sangria can be served immediately or kept refrigerated for a couple of hours before serving.

When serving the sangria use a spoon or fork to put some of the citrus pieces into each glass.

Purple Punch (great for kids' party)

Ingredients (stir and refrigerator until serve; no ice needed):

1   large bottle cranberry juice

1 small can of frozen grape juice

2   quarts pineapple juice
3   cups sugar
1 1/2 quarts water
1 quart Sprite®

Hot Apple Cider

Ingredients:

2 quarts or liters apple juice
1 cup orange juice
1/2 cup lemon juice
1/2 cup brown sugar
1-2 cinnamon sticks
1 tbsp. whole cloves in spice bag

Heat apple juice almost to boiling. Add spice bag
and cinnamon sticks. Simmer 5-10 minutes. Add
orange juice, lemon juice and brown sugar. Heat
and serve. Makes approximately 20 (4 oz.)
servings.

Tip: Keep warm in a coffee carafe or thermos.
Place sign next to carafe so no one mistakes it
for coffee. Make sure you have Styrofoam
cups next to thermos or carafe.

Vampire Punch

Ingredients:

45 – 50 oz. Red Fruit Punch

6oz. Frozen Lemonade concentrate

6 oz. Frozen Grape Juice concentrate

3 cups Lemon Lime Soda

6 cups water

4 small oranges (washed and sliced)

1 small jar cherries

Thaw lemonade and grape juice before making punch (30 – 40 minutes should be enough time). Put punch, lemonade, grape juice, and water into large punch bowl. Just before serving, add lemon lime soda and fruit and/or fake hand or fake bugs.

Creamy Cocoa

Ingredients:

14 oz. sweet condensed milk

½ cup unsweetened cocoa

1/8 tsp salt

1 ½ tsp vanilla extract

6 cups hot water

Mini marshmallows (optional)

In 2-quart glass container, combine all ingredients except marshmallows. Microwave on HIGH 8 to 10 minutes. Stop after four minutes and stir and then resume heating. Top with marshmallows and Halloween sprinkles.

Tip: This cocoa mix can be stored in refrigerator up to 5 days. Mix well and reheat before serving.

For Serving Beer, Bottled Water and/or Sodas

Make your own cooler by carving a pumpkin. I love this idea! It doesn't have to be a tall pumpkin but it needs to be a wide pumpkin. Cut the pumpkin in half and clean out both halves. This creates two coolers: one for beer and one for non-alcoholic beverages. Use a plastic storage bag or plastic wrap as a liner and fill with beverages. Keep large ice cooler beside the drink station and use this as a festive tabletop cooler.

Tip: Fill ice trays with water and add creepy items, such as spiders, eyeballs, or worms before freezing.

More Fun Food Ideas...

Carve out front of pumpkin in design of your choice but make sure it has a big opening. Clean or gut the inside and let dry. Fill with candy! Set on front porch or use as a centerpiece.

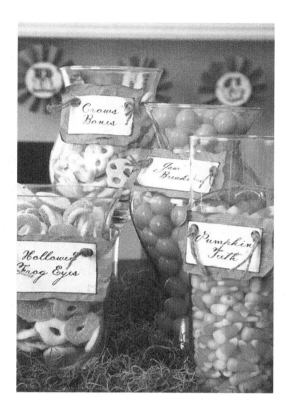

I think this is such a fun idea for any kind of Halloween party whether it is for kids, teens or adults. Simply put candy into different sized jars (any type is okay from mason jars to mayonnaise jars as long as the label has been removed). Add fun labels, such as "Frog Eyes," "Pumpkin Teeth," "Jaw Breakers," and "Crows Bones."

Fun idea, huh? Any size pumpkin will do. Just make skewers of fruit (as pictured) or veggie sticks or different kinds of lollipops or whatever you can think of and insert into the pumpkin. You can draw a cute face or not, depending on your artistic abilities, or you can use a stencil kit or simply put a Halloween mask on the pumpkin.

DECORATING IDEAS

This is my favorite part of Halloween and I tend to go overboard but that can also be attributed to my Type A personality as much as my love of all things Halloween. I buy what I can, make a few easy items, and then spend the majority of my time on the presentation, such as creating a gruesome graveyard and setting up a dazzling party table.

You have to decide before you precede if you're going to have a theme or just decorate as you like. Theme ideas include scary/horror movies/characters (such as Halloween and Michael Myers and Psycho and Bates Motel), Disney movies/characters (such as Haunted Mansion, Tower of Terror and Jack Skeleton from 'Twas the Nightmare Before Christmas), Hocus Pocus, Harry Potter, etc. If you're sticking to a theme, decorating is largely confined to that theme. If you're like me and don't like to be restricted to a specific theme, then you can decorate as you like.

The cheapest and easiest things you can do is go to a party shop, dollar store and/or home improvement store and stock up on the following items and arrange them on tables, mantles, shelves, etc. I always stock up for the next year when they start marking things down 60 – 90 percent. Start looking a few days after Halloween. You'd be amazed at what you can get for a few dollars. For example, I've gotten yard signs that regularly cost $10 or $15 go on sale for 50 cents. Paper plates and napkins that normally cost $1 a pack go on sale for 10 cents.

I have provided dozens of decorating ideas, but you can find more ideas, free Halloween clip art, free patterns for simple DIY projects (such as making your own bats and ghosts to hang or tape on windows and doors) pumpkin carving, and more decorating ideas online by doing a search using keywords "Halloween decorating," "Halloween planning," and "Halloween pumpkin carving ideas."

Here are some quick, cheap, and easy things you can do:

Fall leaves. You can use real leaves out of your yard but fake ones from the dollar store or local craft shop work best because they won't turn brown. They're a good investment as you can re-use them every year for fall season (Sept-Nov). They sell them loose in bags and on strands at most home and dollar stores, seasonally.

Halloween color/theme battery-operated candles.
Place a few of these candles strategically to create nice effect. Best of all, they are not a fire hazard.

Old white sheets. The best part is it doesn't matter if the sheets are stained. This just adds to the effect! Drape these old sheets over furniture like a haunted house. Bonus: It protects your furniture if there are any spills!

Dead flowers. You can usually find black roses in dollar stores around Halloween. I found purple roses last year. I place them strategically in small bud vases with black ribbon tied around the vases. I place one or two of them in front of graveyard markers the way you see fresh flowers in cemeteries.

Colored light bulbs. Replace a few of your regular light bulbs with black or orange or purple light bulbs to create a spooky effect. These are fairly cheap and readily available at most home improvement stores in the lighting section.

String lights. Hang orange and black and purple twinkle string lights all over your porch/living room/dining room/designated smoking area, etc. You shouldn't use overhead lighting during your party. The idea is to minimize bright lighting as there's nothing spooky about that. Instead, use candles, colored light bulbs in lamps, and strings of twinkle lights. These can be found at craft stores and Halloween specialty shops or online. Also, they can be found at most places that sell Halloween decorations.

Halloween CD. You can buy CDs featuring Halloween sounds, songs, and stories at many dollar stores seasonally, as well as other outlets that have a big Halloween section, such as Target. You can also find these CDs online at retailers like Amazon or you can create your own playlist.

Horror movies. I like to put in a classic horror movie (such as Psycho, Scream, and Friday the 13th) during my party. I usually play them without the volume or low volume. It provides the perfect ambience for your festivities. If it's a kid's party, you can play Harry Potter, Tower of Terror, or Hotel Transylvania.

Spider webs. Go crazy with them! Spread them all over the place for super easy and cheap spooky effect. You can buy them by the bag at the dollar store and cut up or tear off what you need for each area. These are typically made of cotton or gauze. Both are fine but I prefer gauze because it works so well hanging over lampshades, tables, mantles, etc.

Insects, bats, ravens, and rodents. A nice effect is to have plastic mice peeking out from the fireplace or a rat situated near a chair or coffee table. Also, you can have a raven or a bat on perched on the porch railing and atop graveyard markers and/or spiders sprinkled all around the interior, porch, and graveyard. It's amazing how much cool stuff you can find at the dollar store. You can buy small ravens, small rodents, and small bats at most dollar stores. If you want a big owl or large raven or giant spider you will have to go to a craft store or specialty store.

Ghosts. What's Halloween without ghosts? These can be inflatable, plastic, paper, cardboard, or fabric. I like to use a combination depending on whether I'm placing in a window or hanging from the ceiling.

Monsters. What's Halloween without monsters lurking about? I have a ten-foot monster cut out that I tape to a glass door. The colorful one-dimensional zombie covers the entire door. I keep a soft night light on in that upstairs room so it looks like a monster is on the loose in my house! It is the first thing that party goers and trick-or-treaters notice when they arrive. Even the mailman and my neighbors have told me how cool it is. I ordered it online a few years ago for $25 and it has proven to be a very good investment. You can buy smaller and much cheaper cutouts of ghouls, ghosts, skeletons, vampires, and witches at most dollar stores, as well as at seasonal Halloween specialty shops, such as Halloween Express. If you're crafty you can probably make your own monster. If you find a full monster figure, you can place it in a porch chair to greet guests or lots of other places, such as seated in one of your dining room chairs, standing in front of a window or by the refreshment table, in your graveyard, or peeking out of your closet.

Skulls. These are cheap and easy decorating tools that are available at most dollar stores. They have normal sized plastic skulls, as well as bags of miniature skulls. Higher quality skulls can be obtained at craft and specialty stores. Be sure to place them strategically, such as on the fireplace mantle, living room shelves, on tables, in your graveyard, and on your porch.

Body parts. These are among my favorite decorating tools. You can find realistic-looking plastic body parts at most dollar stores, as well as specialty stores and craft shops. I usually buy one or two more each year to grow my collection. Be sure to buy an assortment of hands, arms, feet, eye balls, fingers, and skulls. These can be distributed all the same places as skulls. I like putting small body parts, such as eye balls and fingers on party platters!

Streamers. I like to hang streamers where the food and drinks are located. It shows folks where to find them.

Streamers offer a lot of bang for the buck. I bought a couple of rolls of orange and black streamers at the dollar store four years ago and am still using those same rolls.

Balloons. Buy black, white, purple, orange, and white balloons. You can get lucky and find Halloween balloon bags but more likely you'll have to buy a bag or two of assorted colors and hand pick Halloween-colored balloons. Be sure to save the other balloons to use for birthday and anniversary parties. See my balloon decorating image on page 156 for my favorite way to utilize balloons.

Luminaries or lanterns. Place these strategically either leading up to your porch and/or around your deck or patio or designated smoking area or your gruesome graveyard. You can make your own luminaries by using a plastic Halloween pumpkin bucket (buy six at the dollar store). Fill 1/3 full with sand and add a tea candle, votive, battery-operated tea candle, or glow stick). I try to use fake candles whenever possible to minimize fire risks or accidental harm to party goers, especially kids. Also, they are less likely to burn out or blow out. Or you can simply use dollar store Halloween trick or treat bags (these need to be paper not plastic). Crafty folks can collect small, generic paper bags and then draw, paint, or glue Halloween images onto them.

Or you can use lanterns if you have a few on hand. Another option is to save old glass jars (clean and remove labels) and add colored candles or glow sticks. Spread a few leaves or a body part or two nearby and you're done. See my milk jug lights decorating image on page 158 for a unique way to light up the night.

Windows, Doors and Mirrors. I love this trick! Buy or make fake boarded up windows so that the outside of your house resembles a condemned haunted house. I have seen where enthusiasts have used real boards and nails to achieve this effect but I don't like to do that for obvious reasons. Instead, I use poster board to create the illusion of a boarded up window. I have seen affordable cut outs of boarded windows sold online and in specialty shops. Also, you can buy fake police crime scene tape and use for effect. I haven't seen this in the dollar store but I have seen all kinds of fun tape sold on Amazon for less than $5 for a 50-foot roll. There are lots of choices, such as "Fresh Graves Keep Out" and "Party Scene Investigation" and Enter At Your Own Risk." These would be great spread across your front porch or to keep folks out of places you don't want them, such as at the bottom of your stairway to the second floor or the coat room or where you have put Fido for the night or at the top of the basement steps. I'm going to wrap the "Party Scene Investigation" tape

around my house this Halloween! Here's a link to where you can find these:
http://www.amazon.com/s/ref=nb_sb_noss?url=search-alias%3Daps&field-keywords=halloween+crime+scene+tape

Also, you can attach spooky images to all the mirrors in your house (especially bathroom and hall mirrors) so that it looks like a ghostly image has appeared. I bought some in the dollar store year before last and they attach by suction cup so no damage is done to your mirror or window. My images are actually warnings, such as "Caution! Zombie Crossing!" "Boo!" and "Beware!" The latter looks like it was done in bloody splattering so it is great for a bathroom and/or hall mirror. You can also go old school and simply use red lipstick to scrawl warning messages across mirrors and tape homemade signs to windows.

Miscellaneous. I have lots of props I have collected over the years, such as a hand that expands when placed in water. I put this into a large science lab looking jar and it "grows" like 500%. I also have a skull and skeleton that also "grow" so I place them in large jars too. These create cool specimen jars. The trick is to use a large jar as it will only grow as room permits. When Halloween is over, I pull them out of the jars and lay them on top of hand towels to begin the drying out process. This typically takes up to a week for these to go back to their original size. I have been using these same dollar store items for six years and they still look good.

I have a fake arm that appear to be reaching for the closet doorknob, as if trying to get out of the closet. It looks so realistic right down to the fingernails! Also, I have one-dimensional card board figures, like the aforementioned ten-foot zombie. I have lots of colorful signs I use to line the driveway and sidewalk. These are large and small painted wooden signs. They were $10 - $20 apiece but I got them for $1 - $2 buying them the week after Halloween.

I have all kinds of Halloween figurines, a Halloween village, and a Halloween tree. I bought the village at a department store at least ten years ago and picked up the Halloween accessories (figures, trees, and signs) at the dollar store. I bought a black Christmas tree at Garden Ridge about five years ago. It originally sold for $99 but I waited until after Christmas and got it for $29. It was a gamble because items can sell out but I took the risk that not many folks wanted a black Christmas tree and it paid off. It is pre-lit and seven feet tree so it is just what I wanted. I have a combination of handmade and store bought ornaments on it. I have invested in a few unique ornaments that give the tree some pizazz but I not paid more than $10 for any of the ornaments. I have seen some I'd like to have but I refuse to pay $40 or $50 for a Halloween ornament. My tree topper is a two-foot mesh ghost and I drape Halloween ribbon around it haphazardly to finish off the tree.

There is no limit to how much decorating you can do, so these are just ideas or guidelines. You can also use your own imagination and check out your neighborhood and go online for more ideas.

One thing I don't discuss in this book is special effects. You can buy animatronics, such as vampires that raise up out of a coffin or a witch that stirs a cauldron while cackling or chanting a spell. You can buy or rent a fog machine or a fake flaming cauldron. You can buy a doormat that screams every time a guest steps on it. I have a doorbell that says "Enter at your own risk!" when pressed. I've even seen a motorized candelabra that seemingly floats in the air all by itself. I have also seen a figure that lifts his head in the air and then puts it back on his head! There are remote-controlled ghosts and goblins.

There are lots of options, but these aren't necessary and can be expensive and time consuming to set up, which isn't in keeping with our KISS motto. Another thing I don't like is if it stops working (as everything electronic eventually does) you have a very expensive inanimate object. However, if you are into this kind of thing I have to admit they are nice touches. Go ahead and invest in one or two fancy gizmos. Check out www.hauntedprops.com and http://www.frightcatalog.com/halloween-props/animated-props/ for ideas. Be sure to read customer reviews and return policies before buying anything.

Halloween Book Trivia

1. Who wrote the famous spooky tale, *The Legend of Sleepy Hollow*? Bonus: Who is the main character of this story?
2. Who wrote a number of famous spooky stories including, *The Raven*?
3. This famous horror fiction writer's books have sold more than 350 million copies, including *The Shining* and *Under the Dome*. What is this writer's name?
4. This famous American writer is most famous for her series of novels *The Vampire Chronicles*. What's her name?
5. When was the first Amityville Horror book written?

Answers: 1. Washington Irving (Ichabod Crane); 2. Edger Allen Poe (pictured); 3. Stephen King; 4. Anne Rice; 5. *Amityville Horror: A True Story* came out in 1977. It was written by Jay Anson.

Turn your dining room into a creepy cemetery.

What you need:

Black sheets, paper, or fabric

One piece of foam core, poster board, or cardboard for each chair

Textured spray paint

Black acrylic paint and paintbrush

Brown burlap (enough to cover table)

A large skeleton or skeleton parts

Sheet moss

131

Dried leaves

Spider webbing

Plastic spiders, bugs, rats, and bats (get creative and place these creepy party crashers under the dining room table, on the chandelier, beside or on the punch bowl, on platters, etc.)

Black paper plates

Fun/scary goblets or cups

Black utensils

Start by cutting the burlap in wide strips. Layer them on the table. Scatter skeleton bones throughout the center of the table, tucking bones into and under the burlap. Spread moss around the bones and scatter dead leaves. To achieve a sense of foreboding eeriness, stretch thin strands of spider webbing from the corner of the table up to the chandelier or hanging fixture. Encase the chairs with the webbing, too. Create creepiness by hanging spiders from the webbing, suspending bats in flight, and scattering bugs on the table.

Cover the windows with inexpensive black fabric or black construction paper. The goal is to create a very dark room. Use candles and orange and black or purple and black string lights.

To make tombstones: Use foam core, sturdy poster board, or cardboard, trace the shape of a tombstone and cut it out with a serrated knife. Use textured spray paint to create a granite-like tombstone. Allow the paint to dry thoroughly. Then, use black acrylic paint to scratch in scary epitaphs, such as "R U Scared," "C.U. Soon!" and "U.B. Next!" Attach tombstones to the backs of the chairs using tape, or cut small holes in the sides of the tombstones and insert pipe cleaners through the holes and around the chair rails.

Or you can buy readymade tombstones at the dollar store or craft store. Another idea is to cover the back of the chairs with Dracula capes (male) and witches robes (female). You can add accessories if you like, such as a medallion for Dracula and hat or wand for witch. You can get these items cheap when they mark costumes down after Halloween or assemble your own. Another idea is to use old pillowcases to cover the chairs. Epitaphs can be spray-painted or written on the front and/or back of each pillowcase.

Black paper plates are the perfect match for this table, as are ghoulish goblets and black plastic utensils (or you can use Halloween theme utensils). I bought a bag of assorted dollar store plastic rings with assorted designs (spiders, skulls and bats) and use them as napkin rings or you can simply set out napkins to save time and money.

I use black paper napkins from the dollar store, as well as plastic ghoul goblets that look very nice but only cost .50 each. I let guests keep them as party favors, if they want. If they choose to leave them behind I wash them in the dishwasher and keep for the next party.

Coffin Buffet

Make your own coffin buffet table or go online and order one to use as your party table. Believe it or not, there are all kinds of make-your-own coffin sites and instructions available online, such as:

http://www.wikihow.com/Make-a-Coffin

http://diycoffin.com

Just to show you that there is no end to the coffin decorating possibilities, I've included this picture of a coffin couch that is for sale online. How cool is this! http://www.trendhunter.com/slideshow/coffins-and-caskets

Indoor & Outdoor Decorating Ideas

You can go with one theme, such as Harry Potter, Enchanted Forest, Creepy Cemetery, Mad Scientist Lab, Day of the Dead, Rocky Horror, Twilight, or Pirates of the Caribbean. Or you can simply use all kinds of different decorations, which is what I prefer.

Here are some fun ideas:

Make trees come 'alive' by cutting out circles from green craft foam and adding pupils using a black marker. Use double-stick tape to adhere to trees.

Buy different-sized skulls and place on shelves, mantle, or steps to create spooky effect.

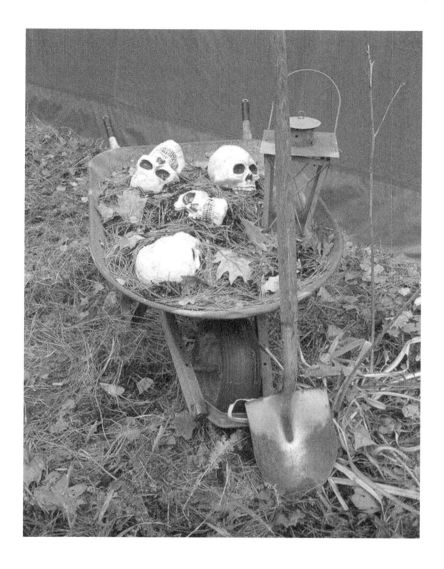

This is so simple and free if you have a wheelbarrow and shovel or someone you can borrow these items from. Position in front of the porch or place next to your graveyard.

Simple and elegant.

Stuff balled up newspapers into the sock and pants leg and add an old shoe or boot. Carve a sinister pumpkin design and insert pant leg into mouth. Use fruit punch or food coloring to look like blood or skip the blood if you have small children who might be scared by it.

I love this! Use black construction paper to cut out this simple design. Bam! Your refrigerator is now a ghost.

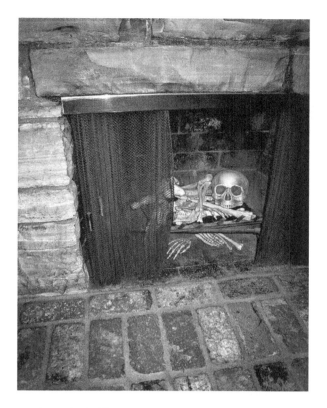

Go to your local dollar store and buy skeleton parts and put them in your fireplace to create spooky fun effect.

Buy a package of self-sticking stenciled letters at any craft store or use colored construction paper to make your own and attach with double-sided tape. Optional: Go online to find traceable patterns to create spider webs, bats, eyes, and pumpkins.

Create your own Sleepy Hollow figure using sticks and
a pole. Attach the sticks using twine and add a pumpkin
head, which can be metal, plastic, or a real pumpkin
that has been gutted and carved. Finish the effect by
adding a cape or cloak. I borrow a seven-foot shovel
from my dad and hide the bottom of it (the shovel part)
in the ground and place a tombstone in front of the top
part of it that remains above ground. I keep the top half
of the shovel above ground to support the lightweight

145

foam tombstone. I place the pumpkin head over the handle end. You can use any garden tool or buy a rod or use an old broomstick, anything that is sturdy, the right size, and weatherproof. I use an old brown burlap sack that I have ripped and cut to fashion a cloak.

Use dollar store spider webs and spiders to drape over lamps, chandeliers, lamp posts, dining room table, porch, and couch for easy, creepy effect.

Fill Halloween-theme tights with fiberfill. Place black
shoes that resemble witches shoes onto feet end of
tights. Use buckles off old shoes or make your own by
using gold paper or paper painted gold and attach to
shoes. Place legs upside down into planter or cauldron.
Can prop a witch's hat and/or broom next to it. You can
also have legs stick out from under your couch, bed,
chair, closet, or porch steps, etc.

Use toilet paper and paper towel rolls to create eyes
watching from your bushes. Use different shapes and
sizes to create different pairs of eyes.

Draw a ghost on poster board and cut out design. You don't have to be a great artist to draw a ghost because you can't go wrong so long as it resembles a ghost. Cut out hole in middle for your front door knob. Add "Boo!" or whatever greeting you like. For the eyes, you can draw them or cut out from magazine or use free clip art and paste onto your ghost. A simple trick is to use two quarters to outline the eyes. Place them where the eyes should be and then cut out, shaving a bit off the side (see picture). You can do this for other doors too to indicate the bathroom or coat room or "Do Not Enter" for rooms where you don't want guests.

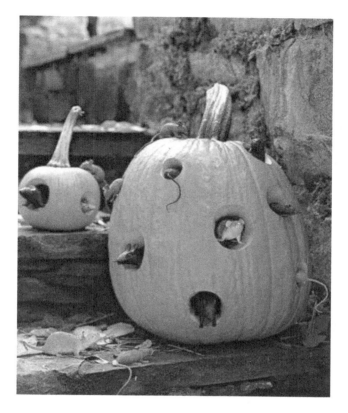

Use a pumpkin carving tool or mallet or knife and ice cream scooper to create holes in pumpkin. Buy plastic mice at the dollar store in different sizes and colors if possible. Note how some are facing out and others have only their tails showing—very realistic looking!

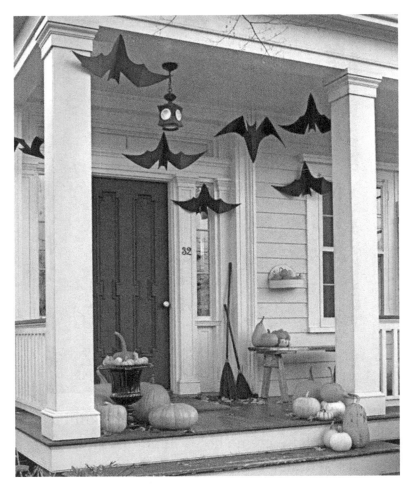

This is easy to do yet creates a colorful and mesmerizing effect. Get a couple dozen pumpkins in different sizes, types, and colors. Scatter a few leaves around the pumpkins and prop some witchy brooms near the door. Make your own bats using traceable designs and black construction paper or buy bats at dollar store or craft store.

You can do more or less, such as adding a raven to the porch railing, a lantern by the brooms, or a Halloween sign on the front door or a cut out on the front window. What I love about decorating is that you can do as much or as little as you like. What I find is that I start out small but keep studying the scene and then keep coming up with ideas until it becomes much bigger and better than I originally envisioned!

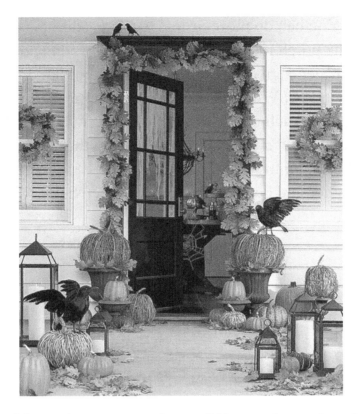

For this project you need two fall wreaths and garland around the door, loose fall-colored leaves, several pumpkins (colored and grapevine), two small and two large ravens, and candle lanterns. You can add or subtract or change the size of anything pictured here, such as no birds over door or add gourds of various sizes and colors instead of using all pumpkins.

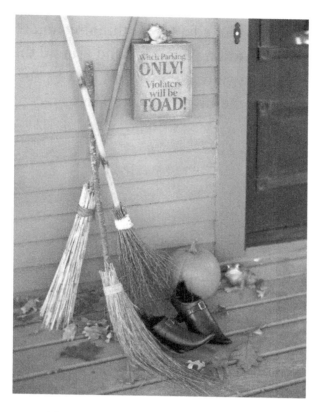

All you need is a pumpkin, two frogs/toads, sign, three
brooms, leaves, and a pair of shoes. I have a pair of
black shoes with buckles that can pass for witches'
shoes. You can find frogs at most home and garden
centers. Scatter some leaves and put out some brooms.
You can get by with two brooms instead of three and
one frog instead of two, if you want to save a bit of
money. You can buy these kinds of brooms at shops
that carry Halloween items or make your own using a
long stick, twine, and grapevine or such. If you have an

old broom, you can adapt it by thinning and reshaping the thistles and adding a twine band around the base. If you can't find a sign like this, just make your own by painting or stenciling a foam board or piece of old wood.

Use alternating black and orange candles with fall leaves under and around mason jars to create lighted path along the sidewalk or up the porch steps and/or up interior steps. Optional: Use two-sided tape to add plastic spiders or bugs to outside of jars.

Buy a package of orange and white balloons and use black marker to draw fun faces on them after you have blown them up. You may have to buy a bag or two of assorted balloons and use only the orange and white balloons, saving the rest for another occasion. Tie strings on them and place balloons around the room(s). You can tie to chairs, railings, and objects.

Bend thick wire (or clothes hangers or picture hanging wire) into handles and use them to hang small jack-o'-lanterns on shepherd's hooks along your sidewalk, around your porch and/or along the driveway. Or you can hang pumpkins from tree branches (and ghosts too) in your backyard if you'll be using your deck during the party.

Save gallon milk jugs until you have what you need (10 – 12 create a nice effect). Wash and air dry jugs. Use a black marker to draw different faces on them. If you leave the caps on while you draw the faces, the jugs won't change shape (dent). Use a craft knife to cut small holes the size of silver dollars in the back of each jug. Get out your strings of Christmas lights or buy some Halloween color low-watt (50 watt) lights. You can find short strands for sale in most dollar stores so you can put a couple of strands in each jug. Place the jugs where you want them and then stuff a couple of strands into each jug, stringing the lights between the jugs. You will probably need an extension cord to run up to the house/porch outlet.

Or instead of light strands you can use glow sticks. I love these because they are so user friendly. No cords or batteries or assembly is required! They are available at most craft stores and can also be found online, such as at www.coolglow.com (40¢ each). Note that you can use different colored sticks for different effects.

Make your own graveyard. This is one of my favorite ways to decorate. The best part is that there is no right or wrong way to do this. You just do what you like. You can even use Christmas lights to illuminate your creepy  cemetery, as opposed to clear or Halloween-colored lights. Depending on how creative you are, you may opt to make some of these props. I prefer to buy them at the dollar store and use the extra time to play around with presentation.

What you'll need:

Tombstones in various shapes and sizes (Note: most are made of Styrofoam and will have to be weighted down somehow. I use small dumb bells behind the tombstones to keep them propped up, but you can use anything you like, such as large rocks or rods)

Skeletal remains (body parts)

Shovel

Wheelbarrow

Partially dug grave

Fencing (make your own or go to the garden shop of local home improvement store or you can sometimes find small plastic fencing in the dollar store or you can borrow fencing from your garden or flower bed)

Flood lights (or creepy orange LED lights or Christmas string lights and extension cord or glow sticks) to be able to see graveyard at night

Fake raven(s)

Ghosts hanging in nearby trees

Creepy signs (keep out, beware, no trespassing…)

Ghouls or monsters

Decide where you want to put the graveyard. It needs to be prominent so your front yard is best, but don't make it too big an area. You want to keep it manageable. I put mine in my front yard near the house rather than near the street. I do this to discourage vandalism or thievery. Unfortunately, there are folks out there who will steal your cool stuff, especially if it is at the street.

Once you decide the dimensions (I recommend something like 12 feet x 12 feet), mark off the area so you know your perimeters. Don't put the fencing up until you're finished so that you have easy access to the area.

Next, dig a partial grave. Leave a pile of dirt beside the open pit, as well as the shovel and wheelbarrow (or you can leave these items just outside the cemetery).

Hang ghosts and/or skeletons in the trees (assuming you have trees in the area).

Post creepy warning signs outside the cemetery. You can buy these or make your own.

Use tombstones and body parts to complete the effect, i.e. a hand or arm sticking out of a grave and a leg sticking out from under the fence. You can go wild and add entire skeletons, scarecrows, zombies, ghosts, witches, and/or animated figures.

Light it up. Use light strands or flood lights or such so that it can be seen at night. If you have bushes and/or trees nearby, you can string lights there rather than in the graveyard. You can use multi-colored lights, Halloween-colored lights or clear lights.

Lastly, put up the fence and set a raven on top of it. I also have a huge spider and spider web that I drape over the fencing to complete the effect.

I want to remind you that I am only offering suggestions. You can do whatever you like. You can have a whole cemetery of zombies or no figures at all. You can add a grim reaper or witches huddled over a cauldron casting a spell. You can light it up or not. You can buy fancy pre-made signs and elaborate tombstones or make your own. If you make your own you need to use foam board and/or wood so that they are weatherproof. The same is true with whatever you put in your cemetery. You can use cut outs of ghosts and ghouls but they are not weatherproof. The same is true for decorations meant to be used inside. The fabric can mildew and ruin.

Pumpkin Carving Tips

Wherever you do this project, be sure to put down newspapers before getting started because this is a messy task. Start by cutting a circle around the stem of the pumpkin so that you can clean it out. Use a sharp, long-bladed knife.
Tip: Cut the top at an angle so that the lid will stay in place. Otherwise, it fall through the hole.
Find the smoothest side of the pumpkin. That's where you want to make your face. Use a free stencil found online: http://www.kraftrecipes.com/recipes/holidays-and-entertaining/holidays/halloween/halloween-party-ideas/pumpkin-stencils.aspx or buy one at the store or create your own design. Tape the paper with your design onto the side of the pumpkin that you have chosen as the smoothest. With a sharp, serrated knife, cut out the design.

As discussed earlier in the book, you can opt to use masks, paint, stencil, or otherwise decorate your pumpkin without having to cut and gut it. Or you can buy artificial pumpkins in different sizes and designs. Most are pre-lit using a battery or power cord.

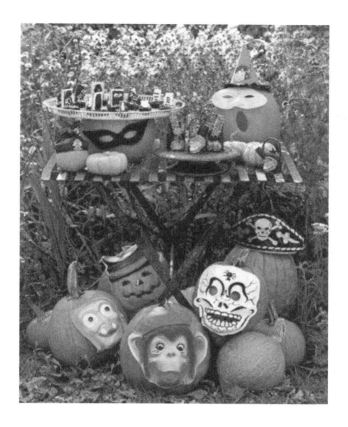

I like this idea because it's so simple (no carving required!) yet creates a dramatic and different look. Buy party masks and/or Mardi Gras masks at the dollar store or party store or make your own and/or find vintage masks to decorate several different-sized of pumpkins.

Boiling Caldron

What You Need:

Hot Water

Large Metal Bowl or Bucket (should be able to fit inside the cauldron) and Large Black Plastic Cauldron

Dry Ice

Heavy Work Gloves and Hammer

Wear gloves when handling dry ice and Set up in well ventilated area. Break the dry ice into five or six inch pieces using the hammer. Put back in the bag it came in and back into the freezer until party time. When it is time, fill metal bowl half full with hot water and set inside caldron. Wearing gloves, take a piece of the five or six inch dry ice out of the freezer and place in the hot water bowl/bucket. The fog will almost immediately begin rolling over the sides of the cauldron. When it dissipates, it is time to add more hot water and another chunk of dry ice to the bowl.

What You Need To Know About Pumpkins...

Real pumpkins will only last a few weeks at most once they have been carved and gutted. <u>To help them last as long as possible, spray a mixture of bleach and water on the inside of your pumpkin daily or coat the inside w/ petroleum jelly to keep mold and dehydration away.</u>

If you don't want to mess with real pumpkins, nice-looking artificial ones are available at most stores during the fall and they are fairly affordable at $10 – 30 each. You can invest in a few pumpkins in different sizes and have them to use for many years to come. I buy ones that plug in because battery-operated gadgets like this tend to use batteries fast. But if you're going to use on a porch or deck you will want the convenience of battery-operated. As always, I buy after Halloween to get the best price. I have gotten huge $30 pre-lit pumpkins for $3. Be sure to get different sizes and shapes rather than a bunch of similar pumpkins.

Another fun fall idea is to gut a real pumpkin (small or medium) but instead of carving and lighting it insert a fall plant, such as potted orange mums into the cavity of the pumpkin. Display your pumpkin flower pot on a porch or refreshments table or hall table.

For Small Children:

A general rule of thumb for successful kids' parties is to have an afternoon party that lasts two hours (three hours max). That allows enough time to play a couple of games, enjoy treat time, and make a craft. There are all kinds of craft kits available at craft stores and lots of free ideas available online. Here are just a few ideas to get you started:

Slime Station. Kids will love this and will talk about making slime long after your party's over. You will be the cool mom that let them play mad scientist!

What you need...

Plain White Glue

Green food coloring

Water

Baby powder

Borax powder

Funnel

Measuring cups and spoons

Mixing bowls and spoons for each child

(2) Plastic 1-liter bottles

Small plastic sealable bags (for storing the slime)

Wet wipes and paper towels

You can do this part in advance:

Goo #1: In one bottle (using funnel), pour 2 cups water, 2 ½ cups glue, ½ cup baby powder, and green food coloring (until mixture is light green). A nice touch is to put a peel off label on the bottles identifying them as "Goo #1" and "Goo #2". The kids will love this and it will be helpful to you.

Goo #2: In the other bottle, pour 2 cups warm water and 2 tablespoons borax powder.

At the party, set up the slime station in a suitable place. Be sure to spread out newspapers all over this area. Keep the group sizes small. Give each child a spoon and mixing bowl. Pour ¼ cup of Goo #1 into each child's bowl. Add 2 teaspoons of Goo #2 to their bowls. Make sure they stir immediately as mixture will become dough-like. Once this happens, they can discard their spoons and use their hands to play with their slimy dough. When they are done, place each goo ball into a plastic bag for the child to keep. If refrigerated, it'll last up to a week or so. Use the wet wipes and paper towels to clean their hands.

Note: To make sure that this comes out right, be sure to slowly add Goo #2 to Goo #1 and stir while pouring. If the mixture becomes hard rather than slimy, you have added too much Goo #2.

Another favorite pastime is **Piñatas**. You can buy Halloween theme piñatas, such as pumpkins, pirates, and ghosts at your local party store and fill it with candy and small party favors (and maybe clues for a scavenger hunt or other party game). If you can't find any locally, check out www.pinatas.com for all kind of options.

Another craft project idea that's fun and easy for kids is painted **Creepy Luminaries**. Save jelly jars, peanut butter jars, mayonnaise jars, etc. Clean thoroughly and dry completely.

What You Need…

Jars

Acrylic paint

Black magic marker

Tea candles or glow sticks

Paint jars using acrylic craft paint in all kinds of fun colors, such as green, orange, and purple. One layer is enough. Two layers may result in peeling. Besides, you're going for the primitive or rustic look. Be sure that paint is completely dry before proceeding. I recommend doing this step before the party so that you don't have to wait to dry or worry about kids getting paint all over themselves and your house.

There are several options for making the face. The kids can simply draw the face freehand and then paint over the outline. Or you can use paper or cardboard to create stencil faces that you trace onto the jar. Or you can simply use a black permanent marker to "paint" faces. I painted the jar rims with black paint. Then let them all dry for about half an hour. Spray with glaze, I use two coats. Let dry for several hours.

After dry, insert a glow stick or tea candle. You can either use a battery-operated tea candle or a real one, but I recommend the battery lights since this is a kids' project. I have ones that change colors and that creates a fun effect. You can, however, use real tea candles and light using a long-stemmed match like the kind used for lighting a gas grill.

For kids between 4 – 10 years old, **Pumpkin BINGO** is a good option. Use pumpkin tokens instead of bingo chips and shape your bingo cards into ghosts. Halloween theme trinkets (or pirate swords and coloring books, etc.) and candy will serve as prizes.

Monster Musical Chairs is another good party game for this age group. Play Halloween songs and line up the chairs. The kids can do the monster mash and walk like Frankenstein (you instruct them each time you restart the music). When the music stops, everyone sits down. The child without a chair is eliminated and so is another chair. Each round involves losing a child and a chair until down to the last child who wins the prize.

Make a Monster. Use toilet paper and paper towel rolls and the following items or any other items you can think of to create your own monster, such as craft paint, ribbons, colored markers, buttons, drinking straws, Halloween theme stickers, feathers, and construction paper. Set up a craft station complete with all these items and give each child one or two rolls. Assist children with any taping or gluing that needs to be done.

Very small children will enjoy **Pin the Nose on the Pumpkin:** Pin the nose on the pumpkin is an easy Halloween game for toddlers to play. To setup the game start by making an adorable pumpkin banner with black and orange felt. Have the kids "pin" the nose on the jack-o-lantern after a few blindfolded spins. The closest to the actual nose wins!

Zombie Apocalypse is another good party game for this age group. It's a Halloween variation of pin the tail on the donkey. To play, you need to create one or go online and find a printable zombie. You can even use a photo of a zombie if you can find one large enough. Sometimes video stores have movie cut outs that they will sell you that you can use instead, such as Michael Myers (Halloween) or Jason (Friday the 13th) or some other vampire or zombie or such. Whatever you end up using, tape it or otherwise secure it onto a garage wall or some other large flat surface. Be sure to cut out a good-sized hole in the head and/or chest beforehand. You'll also need to buy a cheap dart gun at the dollar store that will come with rubber or foam darts. You will find this on the toy aisle of most dollar stores. The child who gets the most shots in to the zombie's head and/or chest wins.

A twist on Zombie Apocalypse is **Untouchable Zombie**. Pick a child to be the zombie. That zombie child lies on his back on the floor or ground. The other children try to wake the zombie from the dead by making it yell or laugh or move BUT THEY CANNOT TOUCH THE ZOMBIE. They call tell jokes or make funny noises or whatever else they like but they cannot come in contact with the zombie. When someone succeeds in waking the zombie, a different child is selected as the new zombie.

Another variation on Zombie Apocalypse is **Zombie Who?** The zombie is blindfolded and the rest of the children must assemble around him/her in a tight circle. Mark a perimeter that the kids cannot go past. Once the zombie touches or tags someone, that child must laugh loudly. If the zombie can identify the child who laughed, they trade places. If not, the game continues until the zombie tags and identifies someone.

Eyeball Race. Another idea that will keep the kids active is a twist on a classic party game. Do you remember the egg race where you had to make it to the finish line carrying an egg on a spoon? This is the same thing but with a plastic eyeball instead of an egg. These can be readily found at a dollar store eyeball or you can use a ping pong painted to look like an eyeball. These can be purchased on the toy aisle of most dollar stores. Each child gets a spoon with an eyeball on it. They must race to the finish line and the first child to make it across the finish line with the eyeball still on their spoon wins. Or you can make it a relay race by dividing the kids into two teams and making the kids "hand off" their spoons to the next child on their team. The first team to make it to the finish line with their eyeball spoon wins. In this version, the eyeball can be dropped but must be retrieved and repositioned before the race can continue.

Halloween Obstacle Course can be lots of fun. Set up a Halloween themed obstacle course in your backyard or other suitable area. The player who makes it through first (or the fastest) wins. I suggest three legs to the race, such as Leg 1: Witches Ride (have children "ride" a broom as fast as they can through this part of the course. Leg 2: Ghosts (have children keep ghost in their hand throughout this part of the race; the ghost will be a white balloon with a magic marker painted face to resemble a ghost; if they lose grasp of the balloon "ghost" they lose) and Leg 3: Tunnel Escape (players must crawl through a makeshift tunnel to escape from a monster; the tunnel can be a large appliance box or a created by stacking hay bales).

Monster Station. Do you remember the party game when you were blind-folded and had to figure out what you were touching? It's a timeless party game and kids love the "gross" factor.

What You Need:

One Dried Pear or Apricot (ears)

Three raw Chicken Thigh or wing Bones (fingers)

One Medium Peeled Banana (tongue)

One small can of large corn niblets or kernels (teeth)

Peeled Grapes (eyeballs)

*Corn Silk (hair)

Small amount of cooked spaghetti (veins)

*There is usually a place in a grocery store near the ears of corn that is a shucking station. You'll find tons of corn silk there.

Set up **Monster Station** in a dark corner and explain to the kids that you have managed to obtain monster body parts from a mad scientist (can even have one of the other adults dress up like a mad scientist complete with goggles, gloves, and a doctor's jacket and "assist" you). Explain that each paper bag laid out on the table (the table should be decorated so as to resemble a monster station, i.e. black tablecloth, vials and measuring cups and science lab kind of stuff) contains a monster body part.

You'll need seven paper bags and seven plastic bowls to hold the aforementioned body parts. The idea is for the kids to guess which body parts they're touching. Store the body parts in plastic zip bags until time for the party. Then transfer the items into bowls and put those into paper bags.

You only want to have the bags open far enough for the kids to stick their hands into, not to be able to see the contents (another reason for the dark or low lit area). You can also loosely tie a ribbon around the bag to prevent peeking.

After they have touched the body parts and made their guess, flip over the card in front of each bag that identifies the part (or you can secure the card inside an envelope and make a big deal out of taking the card out of the envelope and reading the results), such as eyeballs or fingers.

Be sure to have plenty of paper towels and/or wipes available.

Speaking of monsters… how about a **Monster Makeover**? Divide kids into teams of 2 – 4 and give each team a bag of assorted items such as strange hats, makeup kits, false noses, fake warts, wigs, etc. Each team will choose a member of their team to make up or they can draw names or straws to decide. Each team should be given roughly 10-15 minutes to turn the person they are making over into a monstrous looking creature. The host decides on the winner and awards small prizes to that team.

FYI: Some parents opt to rent entertainment, such as clowns, a petting zoo, pony rides, water slide, and/or bouncy house. There is nothing wrong with this but it can be expensive. It is up to you how much you spend but it is not necessary to spend a lot of money or hire characters or animals or such to have a great party.

Older Children:

If the kids are too old for craft stations or games, try storytelling, a costume contest (with a good prize for this age group), and/or scavenger hunt (again, needs to be good prize for winner).

Storytelling. You can read a few stories to them or just tell a few stories to them while they enjoy some Witches Brew (punch) or Witches Milk (hot chocolate) and fudge cookies. They're never too old for chocolate! Make sure the tales are age appropriate (and local/regional stories are always a big hit). Don't share more than three or four stories because they have short attention spans.

Pumpkin Bowling: Pumpkin bowling is another fun Halloween party game for kids or adults. Set up plastic bowling pins or empty plastic bottles filled halfway with water. Use a small to medium-sized pumpkin as the bowling ball. Have prizes like Halloween-inspired toys or candy bags for whoever can knock down the most pins.

For Teens & Adults:

Reading to Teens and Adults does not work, even though they love stories. One suggestion for storytelling is to have someone draw a slip of paper out of a bowl. It will contain the first sentence or first paragraph of a scary story and then let the person who drew the sentence complete the story. Award a prize at the end to the most creative storyteller. Some ideas:

"We were on our way home from a party when we had car trouble on a deserted stretch of road. We had no cell service, but we saw an old Victorian mansion up on the hill and decided to go ask for help…"

"I decided to go camping with some friends. We thought we were going to have a great weekend, but when we got to the park a ranger warned us we should turn around and go home. He told us that a guy had escaped from the insane asylum that was located a few miles away. Authorities believe he might try to hide in the woods…"

"I awoke to find a ghost at the foot of my bed. It appeared to be wearing some kind of military uniform and holding…"

"My friends and I joined a team of ghost hunters to explore the McCreepy Mansion to find out once and for all if it was haunted. We met at midnight outside the gates…"

I've found that teens really get into this and come up with some very creative (disturbing!) stories. A twist on this is to use the card to start the story and then pass the lantern or flashlight to the next person who continues the story until the last guest concludes the story.

Memory Game. This is good activity for all age groups. Show guests several Halloween/Fall items on a tray and set a timer for twenty seconds then remove the tray. Have the guests write down as many items as they can remember. Use items such as a mini pumpkin, a toy black cat, a plastic spider, a piece of candy, mask, etc or get really creative and use a small Halloween sign (with bonus points for remembering what it said) and a horror movie DVD, etc. The person who remembers the most items wins a prize.

Halloween Fear Factor: For this game, blindfold guests and have them put their hand into a bowl or jar filled with something gross to the touch. Then have them guess what they just touched. Some ideas include gelatin, peanut butter, grapes, and crushed Oreos. Award prizes for the people who have the most accurate guesses.

Halloween Trivia: Before the party, make up age appropriate Halloween movie, TV show and general trivia cards, such as these kinds of questions for teens, "How many Friday the 13th movies were there?" "What horror movie series did Jamie Lee Curtis star in? The questions should be about Disney movies and characters for small children.

Who Are You? This is a fun game. Write down characters from famous horror movies (or kids' movies) on a piece of white cardboard and tape onto the back of each guest. Make sure they don't see the answer. Other guests offer clues to help this person find out who he/she is. You can even put a couple of clues on the bottom of each card. Once the person guesses correctly, the ID tag is removed. This doesn't have to be a time limit or planned activity. It can happen throughout the party. Have a small prize (party favor) on hand for each guest to receive. Trade it for their ID tag. The reward will ensure that people will make an effort.

Another idea is **Horror Movie Charades**. Divide the group into teams for a short game of charades where the answers are recent, popular, and/or classic horror movies.

Costume Contests and **Scavenger Hunt**s are good activities for teens and adults too. However, the prizes must be good ones for teens, such as a DVD movie collection (ex. *Scream* trilogy) or Amazon gift cards or movie tickets. Prizes can be silly and inexpensive (like gag gifts) for adults.

Variations on Scavenger Hunts…

Pumpkin Hunt
Hide small decorated pumpkins and gourds around your home for participants to find. This is a fun activity and

the item becomes a memorable party favor.

Pirate Scavenger Hunt

Hide chocolate gold coins or plastic 'gold' coins all over your house or throughout a designated area. Participants will use these to "cash in" for bigger prizes found inside a pirate chest (hide clues attached to the coins to lead them to this chest). The chest will contain party favors which the coins can be traded for, such as pirate paraphernalia, candy, Halloween theme puzzle book, comic book, etc.

Sophisticated Scavenger Hunt (for teens and adults)

Divide guests into teams of 3 – 6 people. Hand out a scavenger hunt list to each team inside a sealed envelope.

You can decide what the items and/or activities will be, such as a black SUV, an orange construction cone, a Halloween house/yard scene that includes a scarecrow, a real or fake tombstone, the team trick or treating at a house other than where the party is being held, a pet wearing a Halloween costume, posing with someone wearing a certain costume (such as ghost or ninja turtle), and Christmas decorations (Be sure to put out a Xmas decoration at your house and see if participants are clever enough to notice), etc.

Each item checked off is good for ten points or can decide own point system, such as awarding more points for more difficult items or activities.

Explain the rules:

1. One member of each team will use a smart phone or camera (many phones have video options so you can ask for video and watch after game ends and that can add to party fun) to take pix of their team standing beside the item and/or doing the assigned activity. Everyone must be in the photo with the only exemption being the team member taking the photo.

2. The first team that comes back with everything on list done wins OR the team with the most things achieved by deadline wins. Suggested duration is one hour from start time.

3. Define the perimeter, such as must stay in neighborhood and/or must stay on foot and obey all laws. Use common sense and be careful of traffic and respectful of home owners and kids trick-or-treating. You may want to consider having everyone participating in the scavenger hunt wearing ID tags and carry flashlights.

FYI: No matter what age, watch your guests and take your cue from them. If guests don't seem to be having fun, move on.

Halloween History

The origins of Halloween can be traced back to the Druids, a Celtic culture in Ireland, Britain and Northern Europe. Halloween was originally called Samhain meaning "end of summer". In ancient Celtic Ireland, October 31st marked the official end of summer and the end of the Celtic calendar. This pagan holiday was also known as All Hallows Eve and dates back over 2,000 years.

It was customary for Druids to perform ritualistic ceremonies and make sacrifices to pacify their gods. They did this with a harvest festival complete with sacrificial bonfires (the word bonfire is derived from bone fires). Typically, they would throw the bones of slaughtered cattle into the flames. These festivals served several purposes, including celebrating the end of the Celtic year and the beginning of a new one.

Also, the Celts believed the souls of the dead roamed the streets and villages at night. Since not all spirits were thought to be friendly, gifts and treats were left out to pacify the evil and to ensure that the next year's crops would be bountiful. It is still common to see bonfires all over Ireland on Halloween night. During this festival, there was dancing, storytelling, and fortune reading.

Halloween costumes also come from the Celtic culture. During Samhain, the Druids wore animal skins and heads to disguise themselves. This was so that evil spirits and demons wouldn't realize they were humans and harm them. Their ceremonies consisted of dancing, telling stories, and reading fortunes.

The custom of leaving gifts and treats out to placate the dead evolved into trick-or-treating.

November 1st is All Saints Day. This is when the Christians tried to convert the pagans. The Catholic Church honored all their patron saints on this special day. November 2nd was when poor people went door to door begging for food on All Soul's Day. They were given "soul cakes," which is a pastry made with currants and bread. The recipients would promise to pray for the dead in return for the soul cakes. Additionally, they might receive money and/or other small gifts or treats.

<u>Ten Scariest Movies of All Time</u>

(according to Entertainment Weekly)

The Shining (1980)

The Exorcist (1973)

Halloween (1978)

Psycho (1960)

Poltergeist (1982)

Evil Dead (1982)

A Nightmare on Elm Street (1984)

The Ring (2002)

Night of the Living Dead (1968)

The Texas Chainsaw Massacre (1974)

Halloween Trivia

1. There is no word that rhymes with orange.
2. Bobbing for apples is thought to have originated from the roman harvest festival that honors Pamona, the goddess of fruit trees.
3. 86% of Americans decorate their house for Halloween.
4. Over 10% of pet owners dress their pets in Halloween costumes. The most popular pet costumes are Harry Pawter, Star Wars ewok, bumblebee, sailor or pirate dog, and tiger for a cat.
5. More than 35 million pounds of candy corn will be produced this year. That equates to nearly 9 billion pieces!
6. 7 out of 10 Americans will celebrate Halloween.
7. Six million adults will be witches this year.
8. Three million adults will be vampires this year.
9. The latest trend is in funny costumes, i.e. food and condiments (such as cupcake, candy bar, and bacon).
10. The National Retail Federation predicts the most money ever to be spent on Halloween will occur this year--$8 billion!

90% of parents raid their children's trick or treat bags

Halloween Quiz

Take this fun quiz and test your Halloween knowledge.

1. What was used as jack-o-lanterns before pumpkins?

   a. Gourds   b. Potatoes   c. Squash   d. Turnips

2. Pumpkins are the same as gourds. True or False?

3. Black signifies night and orange represents pumpkins. True or False?

4. Halloween is the fourth most popular holiday behind Christmas, Easter, Thanksgiving, and New Year's Eve. True or false?

5. How much is spent annually on Halloween decorations, costumes, candy, and parties?

a. $10 million   b. $100 million   c. $1 billion   d. $4 billion

6. What item is most wanted by trick or treaters?

 a. tootsie pops   b. licorice   c. chocolate   d. gummy worms

7. What is it called when a person is afraid of Halloween?

       a. Samhain   b. Ophidiophobia
       c. Claustrophobia   d. Samhainophobia

8. The first U.S. Halloween celebration was held where?

       a. New York City   b. Washington, DC
       c. Memphis, TN   d. Anoka, Minnesota

9. What year was the first U.S. Halloween celebration?

 a. 1921   b. 1931   c. 1941   d. 1951

10. When was the first Halloween card invented?

a. 1920s   b. 1930s   c. 1940s   d. 1950s

Answers: (1). b & d, Children carved potatoes and turnips and then lit them during the Halloween festivities; (2) True. The gourd family includes pumpkins (actually a type of squash), squash, cucumbers and melons; (3) False. Black represents death and darkness while orange represents the autumn harvest; (4) False. Halloween is second only to Christmas, at least as far as money spent. (5) d, $4 billion dollars (some sources indicate that half this amount is spent on Halloween candy alone; (6) c, It is widely debated which chocolate bar is the most popular with Hershey bars, M&Ms, and Snickers as lead contenders, but anything chocolate is the preference for most trick or treaters; (7) d, Samhainophobia; (8) d. Anoka, Minnesota; (9) a, 1921; (10) a. 1920s, more than 28 million Halloween cards are sent each year and roughly $50 million is spent on these greeting cards

8 – 10 correct answers=You rule Halloween!

6 – 9 correct answers=Respectable.

2 – 8 correct answers=You better step it up.

0 – 2 correct answers=Sad!

<u>Ten Best Movies for Kids/Families</u>
(according to Redbook)

It's the Great Pumpkin, Charlie Brown (1966)

Hocus Pocus (1993)

The Nightmare Before Christmas (1993)

Casper (1995)

Pooh's Heffalump Halloween (2005)

Scooby Doo: Halloween Hassle at Dracula's Castle (1984) or any Scooby episode or movie

For older kids:

Beetlejuice (1988)

Monster Squad (1987)

Coraline (2009)

Halloween Fun

Five Fun Ghost Attractions for Families

If you're looking for some spooky fun this fall that the whole family can enjoy, here are a few ideas:

1. **Ripley's Haunted Adventure** (Gatlinburg, TN). Step into this creepy old mansion, if you dare! Live actors lurk throughout this 10,000-square foot attraction. But you don't have to wait until Halloween to have this scary experience since it is open 365 days a year. You do, however, have to be at least six years old. http://www.ripleys.com/gatlinburg/haunted-adventure/

2. **Trolley of the Doomed** (Savannah, GA and Key West, FL). A costumed guide will show you the most haunted places in Savannah from the comfort (and security!) of an air-conditioned trolley. The guide will share stories of specters and spooks that are sure to entertain all aboard. Those who dare can go into one of the most haunted places in Savannah. This tour is the only one that allows access to this haunted house that also features a voodoo room.
www.trollytours.com/savannah/ghosts-tours-savannah.

3. **Ghost Train Adventure** (St. Augustine, FL). This spooktacular train ride departs nightly from Ripley's Museum. The 90-minute ride includes ghostly stops at Castillo de San Marcos, the French Huguenot Cemetery, and The Castle Warden. www.ghosttrainadventure.com

4. **Hearse Ghost Tours** (New Orleans, LA and Savannah, GA) is an interesting and unusual way to explore of one the most haunted cities in America. Participants ride in the back of a hearse while discovering The Cities of the Dead's most haunted sites. This is a memorable experience! The company also offers a cemetery tour. www.hearseghosttours.com

4. **Disney's Haunted Mansion** (all Disney theme parks) Note: It is called the Phantom Manor in Paris, France Disney theme park. Take a fun ride on the Doom Buggy to have some good old-fashioned PG-rated fun. This is my favorite ride

at Disney. www.disneyworld.disney.go.com and www.disneyland.disney.go.com

FYI: To find haunted hayrides, pumpkin patches, and corn mazes, check out:
http://www.hauntworld.com/find_corn_mazes_across_america

Ten Best Halloween Festivals

1. **Jack-O-Lantern Spectacular** (Louisville, KY) involves a walking trail and more than 5,000 carved pumpkins.

2. **Sycamore Pumpkin Festival** (Sycamore, IL) is a weekend of pumpkins, parades, and good old-fashioned Halloween fun.

3. **Keene Pumpkin Festival** (Keene, NH) features more than 30,000 pumpkins! They hold the Guinness Book of World Records for the most lit pumpkins. The festival dates back more than twenty years.

4. **Haunted Happenings** (Salem, MA) is the place for hardcore Halloween enthusiasts. I've been and it's incredible! There is bonfire storytelling, haunted history tours, a Halloween Ball, and all kinds of special events.

5. **Anoka Halloween** (Anoka, MN) is the birth of Halloween in the U.S. It has been dubbed the Halloween Capital of the World. They offer lots

HAPPY HALLOWEEN! | Terrance Zepke

of special events including a great parade.

6. **Great Jack-O-Lantern Blaze** (Croton-on-Hudson, NY) is offered several weekends throughout October and November. Here you'll see some of the most intricately carved pumpkins in America. We're talking about thousands of works of art!

7. **Great Pumpkin Carve** (Chadds Ford, PA) is probably the biggest pumpkin carving contest in the U.S. Typically, there are 50 – 100 artists competing using pumpkins and gourds weighing as much as 500 pounds!

8. **Pendleton Scarecrow Contest** is on my "to do" list as it is a most unusual and festive event. There are more than a hundred scarecrows featured and there is a scarecrow contest.

9. **Jack-O-Lantern Spectacular** (Providence, RI) takes place at the Roger Williams Park Zoo. Visitors will see lots of animals and spectacular jack-o-lanterns throughout the zoo. This is great event for kids and families.

10. **Hallowe'en at Greenfield Village** (Dearborn, MI) has lots of costumed characters, pumpkins, and festivities.

For more ideas about places to go and things to do this Halloween, visit my Pinterest Halloween board, www.pinterest.com/terrancezepke

Halloween Monster Trivia

1. What is the name of the supernatural creature, in Latin American folklore that drinks the blood of animals – usually chickens and goats?
2. True or false. Vampire Bats were named after vampires.
3. Bobby "Boris" Pickett composed this holiday hit in 1962. What is the name of the song?
4. What is the supernatural condition called whereby a human transforms into a wolf?
5. This creature is believed to inhabit forests, mainly in the Pacific Northwest region of North America. What its name?

Answers: El Chupacabras; 2. True; 3. *The Monster Mash;* 4. Lycanthropy; 5. Bigfoot or Sasquatch

Ten Scariest Manmade Haunted Houses in America

1. The Dent Haunted Schoolhouse (Cincinnati, OH) is reportedly haunted by a real ghost named Charlie. In addition to the haunted house, there is a maze.
http://www.frightsite.com/

2. Nightmare on 17th Street (Cheyenne, WY) has lots of scary theme rooms, such as Texas Chainsaw Massacre and Dead Silence (think evil puppets).
http://www.nightmareon17thstreet.com/

3. 13th Floor Haunted House (San Antonio, TX; Phoenix, AZ; Denver, CO). This is one of the only haunted houses that I'm aware of that has real snakes and other creepy creatures.
http://www.13thflooraz.com/

http://www.13thfloorhauntedhouse.com/

http://www.13thfloorsantonio.com/

4. Edge of Hell (Kansas City, MO) is inside a five-story old warehouse filled with nearly 50 eerie characters ready to give you the scare of your life! The attraction ends with participants shooting down a slide into "Hell!" http://www.edgeofhell.com/

5. Pirates of Emerson (Pleasanton, CA) is actually six haunted houses: Pirates of Emerson, Wicked Wild West, Habitat of Hags, Mental Maze, Doll Hostel, and Lockdown. www.piratesofemerson.com

6. Scream World has five scary attractions, including Outdoor Zombie Graveyard and Slaughter House. www.screamworld.com

7. Blood Manor (Manhattan, NY) features Killer Klowns, DisGraceland, Wall Crawler in Death Row, Cabaret of Death, Graveyard of the Doomed, and Zombie of the Apocalypse. http://www.bloodmanor.com/

8. Netherworld (Norcross, GA) offers spectacular special effects, robotics, and live performers. www.fearworld.com

9. Scare House (Pittsburg, PA). With features like "Delirium 3-D" and "Zombies," how can it not be the perfect haunted attraction? http://www.scarehouse.com/

10. Erebus Haunted House (Pontiac, MI) is in the Guinness Book of Records as the largest haunted house in the world. http://www.hauntedpontiac.com/

Titles by Terrance Zepke

For more information on these titles or to subscribe to my ***MOSTLY GHOSTLY*** blog, visit

www.terrancezepke.com

Ghost Books:

Spookiest Lighthouses (Safari Publishing)

Spookiest Battlefields (Safari Publishing)

A Ghost Hunter's Guide to The Most Haunted Places in America (Safari Publishing)

A Ghost Hunter's Guide to The Most Haunted Houses in America (Safari Publishing)

A Ghost Hunter's Guide to The Most Haunted Hotels & Inns in America (Safari Publishing)

The Best Ghost Tales of South Carolina (Pineapple Press)

Ghosts of the Carolina Coasts (Pineapple Press)

Ghosts and Legends of the Carolina Coasts (Pineapple Press)

The Best Ghost Tales of North Carolina (Pineapple Press)

Ghosts of Savannah (Pineapple Press)

Ghosts of the Carolinas for Kids (Pineapple Press)

Travel Guidebooks:

The Encyclopedia of Cheap Travel: Save Up to 90% on Lodging, Flight, Tours, Cruises and More! (Lookout Publishing)

Coastal South Carolina: Welcome to the Lowcountry (Pineapple Press)

Lighthouses of the Carolinas (Pineapple Press)

Coastal North Carolina (Pineapple Press)

Terrance Talks Travel: A Pocket Guide to South Africa (Safari Publishing)

Terrance Talks Travel: A Pocket Guide to African Safaris (Safari Publishing)

Terrance Talks Travel: A Pocket Guide to Adventure Travel (Safari Publishing)

Terrance Talks Travel: A Pocket Guide to the Florida Keys (including Key West & The Everglades) (Safari Publishing)

Other Titles:

Happy Halloween! Hundreds of Perfect Party Recipes, Delightful Decorating Ideas & Awesome Activities (Safari Publishing)

Lowcountry Voodoo: Tales, Spells and Boo Hags (Pineapple Press)

Stop Talking & Start Writing Your Book (Safari Publishing)

Stop Talking & Start Publishing Your Book (Safari Publishing)

Stop Talking & Start Selling Your Book (Safari Publishing)

Kids Books:

Pirates of the Carolinas (Pineapple Press)

Pirates of the Carolinas for Kids (Pineapple Press)

Lighthouses of the Carolinas for Kids (Pineapple Press)

See the next page for a special preview of one of the books in Terrance Zepke's popular 'most haunted' series:

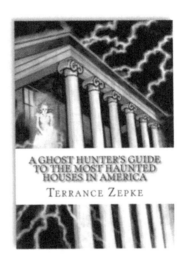

A GHOST HUNTER'S GUIDE TO THE MOST HAUNTED HOUSES IN AMERICA

Korner's Folly House

FUN FACTS:

The structure has been dubbed "The Strangest House in the World."

The house has been officially certified as "haunted" by as many as four ghosts.

The first private theater in America was inside this house. The theater, Cupid's Park, still exists.

The History

The Strangest House in the World. That's what it was once called by an architectural magazine, *Preservation*, and the name stuck. It's no wonder it's considered such a strange dwelling. It is a three-story house that has seven levels. The 6,000-square foot Victorian mansion has twenty-two rooms with ceiling heights ranging from six feet to twenty-five feet. There are many unusual murals and artwork in the house, as well as a unique air distribution system. Another unusual feature is the smoking room. Accidental fires posed a serious threat in those days. With that in mind, a fireproof room was built onto the house. This is the only place that smoking was permitted within the house. No two doorways are the same. The same is true for the fifteen fireplaces. There are numerous cubbyholes and trapdoors throughout the odd house.

The house was the architectural vision of one man, Jule Gilmer Korner. He began building the house in 1878. Two years later, he moved in but continued to make changes to the house for many years. It was built to showcase his interior design business, but later it became a home for his family.

He hired a freed slave to run his household. She affectionately became known as 'Aunt Dealy.' She took good care of the house and Jule until he got married in 1886. After that, the job fell to his new wife, Polly Alice Masten Korner. A cottage was built behind the house and Aunt Dealy moved out of the main house and into this outbuilding.

Jule and Polly had two children. Child-sized rooms were constructed to accommodate them. Many other changes were made, such as the additions of a ladies sitting room and a library. The top story of the house was made into a children's theatre, Cupid's Park. Puppet shows, plays, and recitals were held here for all the children in town to enjoy. Theatrical productions are still produced here on occasion. Underneath the theatre is a huge room that is known as the Reception Room. This is where Jule and Polly did most of their entertaining.

Cupid's Park Theatre (top floor of house)

Because of its odd design and never-ending renovations, a visiting cousin once remarked that "This will surely be Jule Korner's folly." Instead of being offended, Jule was amused. He promptly had a plaque made that read "Korner's Folly" and hung it outside the front door.

Jule Korner died in 1924. Right up to his death he was still working on the house because he never felt that it was finished. Polly died ten years later. The property stayed in the family until the 1970s when it was turned over to the non-profit group, Korner's Folly Foundation.

The Hauntings

Korner's Folly has been investigated by several ghost groups and certified as officially haunted. I have spent the night inside the house, along with an investigative team from the Winston-Salem Paranormal Society. We hunkered down for the night in various rooms across the house, which were reportedly the most haunted areas. These included the Reception Room, Cupid's Park, the ladies sitting room, and one of the bedrooms.

The most haunted area of the house is believed to

be the Reception Room, so this is where I chose to be. The psychic and a lead investigator were also in the room with me. The bulk of the monitoring equipment was set up here, so we could see what was going on in other parts of the house. The director of the foundation, Bruce Frankel, had given us a private tour and implicit instructions regarding our overnight stay. One of the rules was not to touch the furniture, so the three of us were seated in folding chairs in the middle of the room. Beside me was the "kissing couch." It has an "S" shape so that the man and woman can sit on opposite sides and face one another to talk or steal a kiss.

At one point in the evening, I suddenly felt very cold and got a weird sensation. As I was trying to figure this out given that it was a hot June night, I felt something on my arm. Startled, I soon realized that it was the hand of the psychic, who was seated next to me. He spoke softly, "I thought you should know that I sense a female presence on the kissing couch." I quickly processed what he was saying. A ghost was beside me!

She moved around the room, standing next to the piano and near the doorway before she disappeared. I knew when she had moved away from me because the cold (and weird) feeling disappeared as suddenly as it had occurred.

We had some questionable EVPs and one of the team members felt a pinch on her behind when no one was standing near her. That was believed to be the spirit of Jule, who had a reputation as a "ladies man" before he got married. He has been known to pinch female visitors on the behind sometimes during their tours.

Another group, Southern Paranormal and Anomaly Research Society (SPARS), certified the house as being "officially haunted" at the conclusion of their investigation. They picked up lots of EVPs of moaning and "peek-a-boo," which was a favorite game of the Korner children. The group also saw unexplainable shadows and orbs on their images.

If all the reports are true, then Korner's Folly is haunted by several spirits. These include Jule Korner, his kids, and Aunt Dealy and/or Polly Korner.

(Wide angle view of the haunted ballroom and kissing couch)

Visitor Information

The house is open to the public for daytime tours. Also, special events are held throughout the year. The biggest and best is its Holiday Open House. During December, the house is decorated to the hilt, usually by professional interior designers. Take it from me, the house looks properly festive. Jule Korner would be proud!

413 S. Main Street

Kernersville, NC 27284

Kernersville is 2.5 hours from Asheville, NC (155 miles); 7 hours from Columbus, OH (390 miles); and 10.5 hours from Memphis, TN (650 miles).

www.kornersfolly.org

Index

U

Untouchable Zombie
  Activities, 181

V

Vampire Punch, 109
vampires, 124, 129, 198,
  209
vintage masks, 167

W

witches, 82, 124, 134, 148,
  155, 165, 198

Z

Zombie Apocalypse
  Activities, 180
Zombie Punch, 101
zombies, 124, 165

Dear Reader,

Thank you for buying or borrowing **HAPPY HALLOWEEN! Hundreds of Perfect Party Recipes, Delightful Decorating Ideas & Awesome Activities.** I had so much fun creating this book, as you can imagine! I hope you get a chance to try some of these recipes and decorating tips whether it's just for you and your family or for a Halloween party you're hosting.

I spent a great deal of time compiling this information into what I believe is an easy-to-read, useful reference. I would love to hear from you if you'd like to post a question or comment about this book or anything related to Halloween on www.terrancezepke.com. I do respond to all comments. While on my site, you should check out GHOST TOWN and be sure to sign up for my *Mostly Ghostly* blog. As a bonus, you will receive a FREE 50-page Ghost Report when you sign up!

I would also like to ask you to please share your feedback about this book on Amazon or your favorite bookseller so that other readers might discover this title too.

Authors appreciate readers more than you realize and we dearly love and depend upon good reviews! If you've never posted a review before it is easy to do...just tell folks what you liked or didn't like about this book and why you (hopefully) recommend it.
http://www.amazon.com/Terrance-Zepke/e/B000APJNIA/ref=sr_ntt_srch_lnk_3?qid=1438800300&sr=8-3

Thank you again for your interest and here's hoping you have the best Halloween ever...

Terrance

Safari Publishing

Made in the USA
Middletown, DE
16 September 2019